Springer

Berlin
Heidelberg
New York
Barcelona
Budapest
Hong Kong
London
Milan
Paris
Santa Clara
Singapore
Tokyo

Ulrich Sendler

CAD&Office Integration

OLE for Design and Modeling
A New Technology for
CA Software

With 48 figures, including 5 color pages

 Springer

Ulrich Sendler

Haydnstraße 9
D-69121 Heidelberg, Germany

Translated from the German by Intergraph (Deutschland) GmbH, Ismaning

Title of the Original German Edition:

CAD & Office Integration
OLE für Design und Modellierung –
Eine neue Technologie für CA-Software
© Springer-Verlag Berlin Heidelberg 1995

ISBN 3-540-60292-5 Springer-Verlag Berlin Heidelberg New York

Library of Congress Cataloging-in-Publication

Sendler, Ulrich, 1951-
    CAD & office integration: OLE for design and modeling--a new
technology for CA-software / Ulrich Sendler.
        p.   cm.
    Includes bibliographical references and index.
    ISBN 3-540-60292-5 (hardcover)
    1. Object-oriented programming (Computer science)   2. Computer
-aided software engineering   I. Title.
QA76.64.S418   1996
670'.285'57--dc20   96-18686
                                                        CIP

© Springer-Verlag Berlin Heidelberg 1996
Printed in Germany

The use of general descriptive names, trademarks, etc. in this publication does not imply, even in the absence of a specific statement, that such names are exempt from the relevant protective laws and regulations and therefore free for general use.

Cover illustration: Flatiron-Gebäude - Bildagentur Schuster, Oberursel
Cover Design: Künkel + Lopka Werbeagentur, Ilvesheim
Production Editor: Ulrike Stricker, Springer-Verlag, Heidelberg
Dataconversion by Springer-Verlag, Heidelberg
SPIN 10484824   33/3142 – 5 4 3 2 1 0 – Printed on acid-free paper

Preface

If you have monitored the progress of software development over the years, you will already be familiar with
its cycles: phases of gradual enhancement and refinement
of existing technologies are followed by great leaps forward which take it up on to a new plane, where a new phase
of development starts.

At present, though, we are experiencing a regenerative *Giant leap*
leap which in its scope is likely to put all its predecessors
in the shade.

This time we are not simply seeing a new type of *End of an era*
graphical software application or some run-of-the-mill
enhancement in functionality or performance. The new
star is an object technology which is on its way to putting
an end to the era of proprietary CAD/CAM applications
and platforms.

That is the subject of this book. It aims to help you *Fundamentals*
understand the foundations and chief features of this
technology and appreciate what it has to offer to users and
developers of technical applications and what overall
changes will result from this quantum leap for end users
in industry and for the software market.

OLE is the magic word that for some time has been *Spanish it isn't*
haunting the pages of the computer trade press. It stands
literally for *Object Linking and Embedding,* but it has now
taken on a life of its own, and it refers to far more than just
the original functionality.

OLE is a central pillar of Microsoft's strategy for
Windows and Windows NT. It is the heart of an object-
oriented technology, still relatively new, that since the
release of Windows 3.1 has allowed PC users to utilize the
functionality of different applications, simultaneously and
with a previously unattainable ease, within one and the
same document; and the applications can even come from

different vendors and feature different programming languages and different data formats.

From Office to Office

The various Microsoft Office packages are a visible expression of this concept, but it now embraces countless application systems which exist quite independently of Microsoft or any other office solution.

Upgraded

OLE for Design and Modeling Applications is the name of an enhancement which now extends this mechanism to the technical field. It removes from OLE a number of constraints which had only minor consequences for office automation but were totally unacceptable when it came to working with physical models such as are created with modern 3D CAD systems. It might be more accurate to say that it adds to OLE a series of rules and tools which make the technology fully suited to use in product development applications as well.

Building a bridge to the commercial side

The full significance of the enhancement does not stop there, of course. In some respects the new opportunities now opening up within technical applications are themselves less important than the fact that there is now a concept which brings enterprise-wide use of highly disparate applications out of the realms of utopia into the real world.

Using design department parts lists in the purchasing department; applying commercial or process-related information as input data for product development; utilizing a standard word processor for notes on a drawing; having access to a spreadsheet program when creating a header for a drawing; and above all working simultaneously with a number of different technical applications without the tiresome problem of inadequate interfaces for data transfer – in a few years these could all be quite normal scenarios in many sectors of industry.

Enterprise-wide integration in sight

The significance of OLE for D&M (or OLE4D&M or OLE4DM, as the extensions are also known in short) is not just that it allows you to work with different technical applications at the same time. It is that for the first time it opens the door to enterprise-wide integration of all the installed software systems – only where that makes sense and is necessary, needless to say.

These OLE extensions were defined by Intergraph. The project, code-named Jupiter, has been pursued at maximum priority in recent years, and when it was first announced, it gave fresh impetus to the public debate on object technology. Unfortunately, this debate is all too often not founded on any practical understanding of what is meant by object-oriented system development, not to mention object-oriented applications. Everyone bandies about the latest buzz-words that proliferate around the topic, and it is not always easy to find out what they really mean.

OLE4DM demands more intensive study

We have encountered this phenomenon at various turning points in the history of CAD. The availability of the first interactive 3D CAD systems, for example, triggered a profusion of 3D functions which suddenly, and quite unexpectedly, were to be encountered just about everywhere – in the adverts, at least.

The me-too mentality

Personal Computer Operating Systems 1996

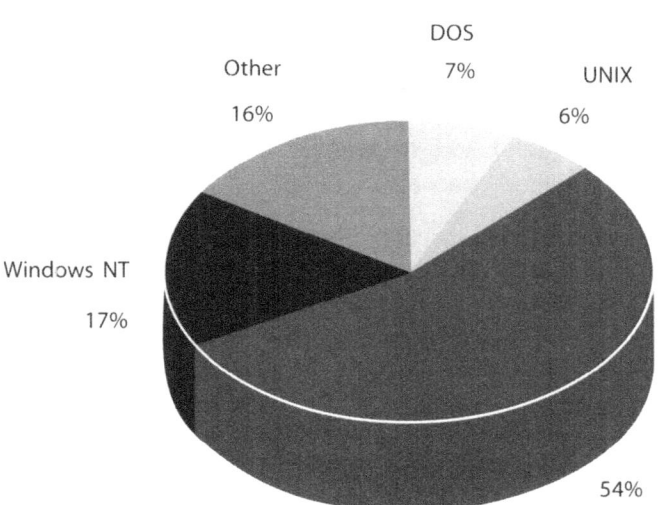

Figure 1: *"The chart is based on the Dataquest projections of future market share for the major operating systems."*

General trend

In truth, a number of software vendors have evidently hit on similar approaches more or less in parallel with developments at Intergraph. Computervision is developing PELORUS, Matra Datavision is offering CAS.CADE/SF, and there are others who are keeping their new designs under wraps.

However, the primary aim of this book is not to examine the latest products to appear on the market, but to discuss the OLE mechanism and its extensions, because, thanks to the 75-million-strong presence of Windows, OLE looks set to become the international standard for future software platforms.

The outlook – sunny for some, gloomy for others

Dataquest has recently published the results of a study predicting to IBM that the release of Windows 95 in the last quarter of 1995 may signal the end of activities on the OS/2 front. And to Apple that its only hope of survival is to turn the PowerPC into a Windows platform. According to the German trade publication "Computer-Magazin", market researchers are anticipating sales of 33.3 million units of Windows 95 in the fourth quarter of 1995 alone. Among the central components of the future Windows operating system are COM (Component Object Model) and OLE.

Origins

Yet what really is object technology? How did it develop into the tool which is now the focus of so many hopes and is giving the whole market something of a shake-up? And how is it related to the overall course of CAD/CAM/CAE and GIS history? The first chapter of this book, intended both for developers and particularly for non-developers, aims to provide general orientation of this type, to explain terminology, and to describe the nature of the problems.

OLE 2.x

The second chapter takes a far more concrete line. To understand and appreciate the significance of OLE in the technical environment we must first take a look at the principles underlying the basic OLE/COM mechanism, at how and why it has become central to Windows, and at what it has been capable of doing ever since 1993 - even if most users know nothing about it and in some cases probably would rather not know. (If you are familiar with

OLE and the principles of object-oriented programming you can skip the first two chapters if you wish.)

Readers will then be in a position to put OLE for D&M into the overall picture. In the third chapter I have tried to walk a tightrope between on the one hand packing in enough information for software developers to gain an idea of the potential role the mechanism can play in their future work and on the other hand not getting so bogged down in details that ordinary users are frightened into shutting the book and never opening it again. For developers, though, the Appendix includes the full specifications of OLE for D&M in the original version published by Intergraph. (Author's comment regarding the English translation of this book: The specifications printed in this book are from December 1995 and are the most recent at the publication date i.e. April 1996; they have been extended and improved since the first version from the beginning of 1995. In the book reference is only made to the original specifications, later revised editions will refer to new additions.)

OLE for D&M

Apart from the actual extensions to OLE, which are available to anyone free of charge, Intergraph has designed other methods which help solve specific problems with technical applications in the context of the OLE mechanism. Some of these relate to application-internal matters, others to orderly interaction between different applications. These aspects are the subject of the fourth chapter.

Additional requirements

The fifth chapter looks at how Intergraph and other design teams and individual developers go about turning the new technology into new products. What makes up a development platform under OLE for D&M? And what does the actual application programmer need to do?

Platforms

The sixth chapter provides concrete examples based on OLE-capable Intergraph products to demonstrate what the results can look like from the end user's perspective.

Sample products

Finally, the last part is devoted to the medium- and long-term prospects arising from a new generation of OLE-based products.

I believe I have kept faith with my principle of presenting technical subject matter in a form that is also comprehensible to non-experts. However, I do feel that it will be essential for everyone to keep up with developments in the years to come, as otherwise we will be left with a handful of initiates who are the only ones capable of understanding what they are seeing and hearing at system demonstrations.

In this book I have done my best to widen the circle of initiates both in Europe and in the USA.

Major support

The book would never have come to fruition without considerable support from people from everywhere at Intergraph who have given me a profound insight into questions of development and strategy. I would like to take this opportunity to express my gratitude for their assistance. I particularly wish to thank Dr. Gunter Oesterhelt and Thomas Weissbarth, with whom I had detailed conversations in which they patiently helped me to a clearer understanding of the nature of OLE and OLE for D&M.

Object of desire

In the interests of users I hope that new-style object technology and the potential of greater interoperability will take root, regardless of the shape they take and the products involved, so that the benefits of modern software are no longer restricted to isolated communities.

Ulrich Sendler, Heidelberg

Contents

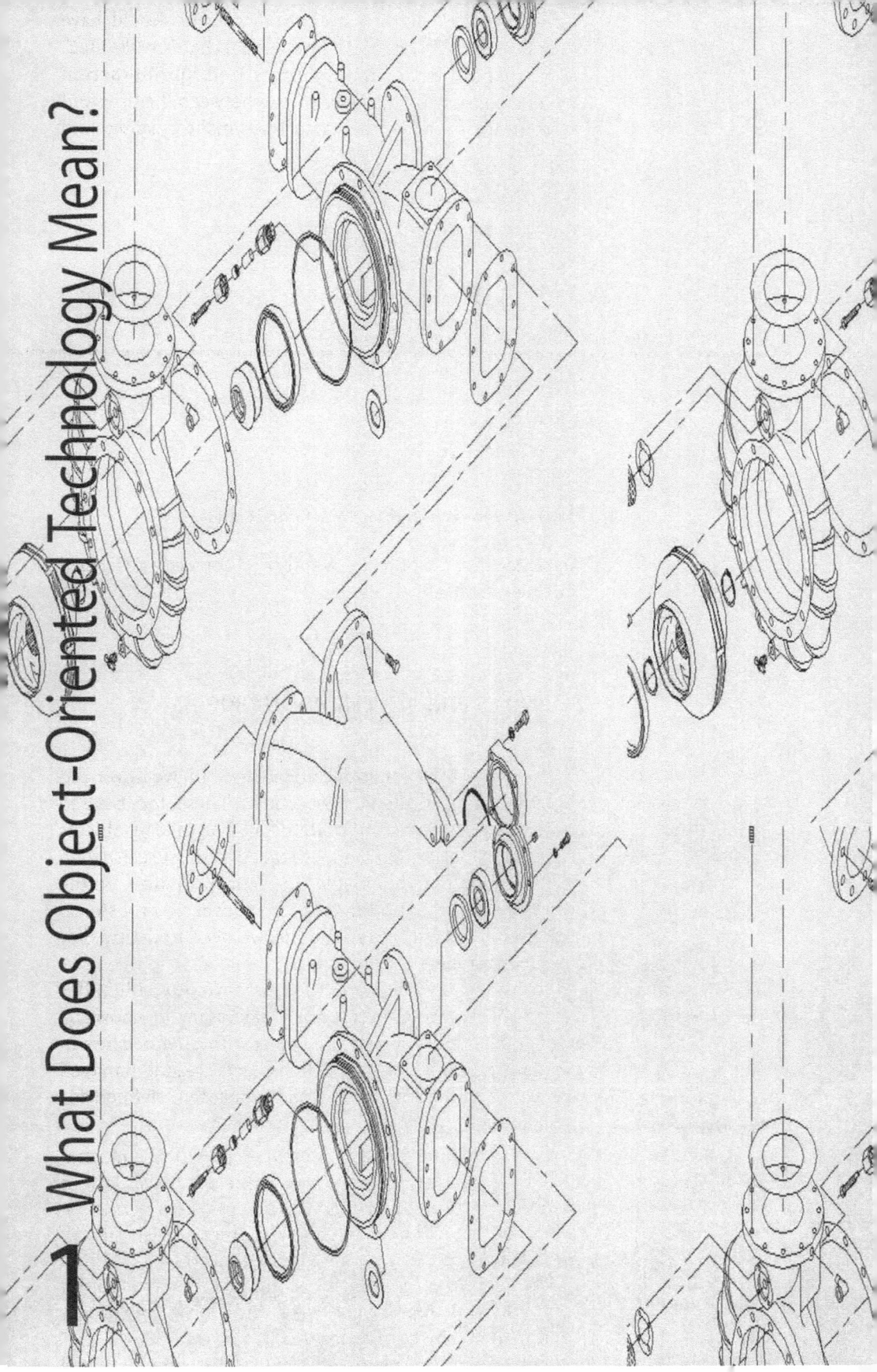

1 What Does Object-Oriented Technology Mean?

1 What Does Object-Oriented Technology Mean?

Before turning to the specific forms that object technology takes in MS-Windows OLE and to its enhancements for the purposes of CAD, we ought to take some time to get our bearings. We cannot properly assess the latest developments without knowing something of the context of the technology as a whole and the way it has developed.

1.1 The Long Road to Objects

From the first computer programs to today's object-oriented systems, it has been a long and winding road full of wrong turns and blind corners. As a theoretical construct, the goal is almost as old as software development itself. Even practical implementations in the form of market-ready products already have a history of over ten years of development. The motivation behind it has been provided both by practical end-user requirements and by inherent forces which exerted growing pressure on developers.

As old as CAD

In the beginning was the procedure. The first software generations were characterized by programs which simply ran through from beginning to end, and all the user could do was enter selections at the keyboard to choose from among predefined alternatives. Everything was essentially predetermined by the programmer, with the user simply governing the actual course of events. As

Keep it all in sequence

the available choices grew more complex, it naturally became more difficult to think through all the different ways the program could run, to identify every conceivable source of error, and to guarantee crash-free program execution.

Between ease of use and unpredictability

Structured programming was really nothing more than an attempt to counter this growing problem by breaking the software down into the smallest possible modules and by making the clearest possible distinction between functions and data. This became all the more essential as programs grew more and more interactive under the pressure of mass use, since the consequence was that the user had more possible actions to choose from, thus making it even harder to predict how the program would actually run.

Awkward procedures

More complex equals more complicated?

So it became clear that the procedural approach to writing software would soon come up against insurmountable barriers – and the more complex the application, the sooner that time would come.

Moreover, using conventional programming techniques, only certain conditions could be represented as the results of analyzable processes and translated into algorithms. This does not reflect the real world, and it conflicts with the demands of users.

Development chain

An example from the field of mechanical CAD: product development breaks down into various phases which traditionally ran consecutively (and that, unfortunately, is generally still the case today). Typically, these phases are: concept, design, drafting, detailing, analysis, prototyping, and manufacturing setup.

Unsatisfactory patchwork

There is as yet no single system capable of satisfactorily supporting this entire development process consistently. The available systems all cover sections of the chain of various lengths. The greater the area covered, the more difficult it is to maintain consistency. The reason is simply that complex structures of this type, not being wholly predictable, exhibit a behavior which is totally

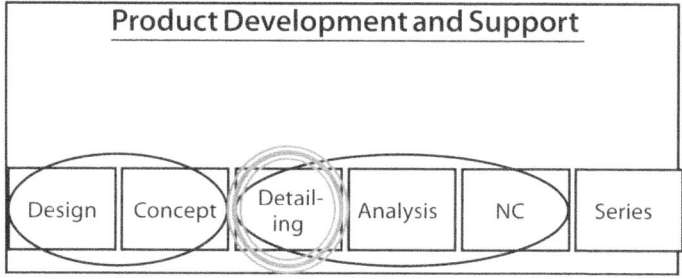

Figure 2: "Most CAD systems primarily support the detailing phase and the preparation of production drawings. Analysis and NC processing may be included if 3D work is involved. If software is used at the concept and design phase, as a rule it is not the same as that installed for the other phases, but as a special package, such as Alias, or CDRS."

irreconcilable with conventional methods of software development. It is impossible to analyze and program the order of individual steps in the development process, to say nothing of the relationships between the various elements, parts and assemblies.

Hence, it was never even remotely possible to accurately simulate products, let alone real-life processes using the old methods.

Perhaps the armed forces wanted a GIS application that could handle radar-relevant objects, not just geometrical elements; perhaps the facility management people in the building trade had to be able to map not just 3D buildings but also the entire infrastructure and production facilities; perhaps CAD-generated models needed to be used for production and analysis. Everywhere developers and users were encountering harsh restrictions which could not be dismantled with the existing tools.

Conventional CAD constraints

An answer to these problems, which were frustrating for vendors and customers alike, seemed to be promised by the object-oriented approach. Now there are many signs that the solution has been found and that what remains is to refine it and turn it into practical application programs.

An end in sight?

Redesign is not enough   However, the solution looks considerably different to what was originally envisaged. It is not a question of thoroughly redesigning the systems using object-oriented programming languages and methods. That has been attempted, and the results are promising. Many systems designed on that principle are now available, and in many individual functionalities they are superior to their predecessors. Yet the heart of the problem has not been addressed, so the old restrictions are all the more painfully evident in this new guise.

The solution is also not a matter of evolving a single, standardized programming language, even if one of the languages in use today were in the long run to become established as the one and only language.

Evolution of Object-Oriented Systems

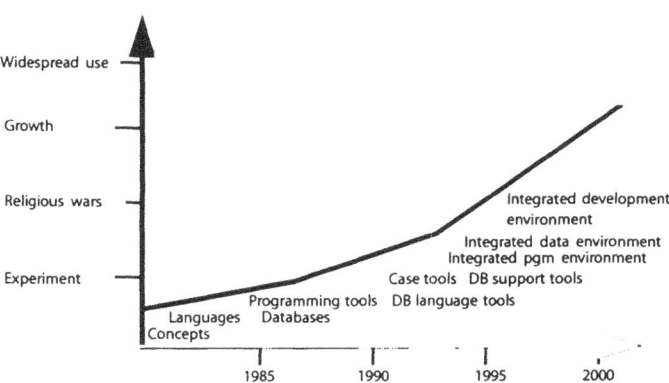

Figure 3: "This graph illustrates the development of object-oriented systems since the end of the 1960s. One interesting point is how database and programming language concepts have merged into integrated development environments. The systems really came of age some time in the early 1990s." (Figure 22 – from a speech given by Dr. Oesterhelt, November 1990)

The object at the heart of the system

I n fact, the true philosophers' stone has turned out to be the extension of object technology *beyond the bounds of individual applications* on a consistent basis. In other words, the object concept is integral to the application environment and to the operating system itself.

Object technology in the operating system

The developers of CAD/CAM/CAE programs cannot claim to have been the first to see the light. The idea has to some extent already been put into practice in other fields – office automation and document creation and management – and the results are currently hard at work on behalf of millions of users, in the form of Microsoft's Office packages, for example, and other systems for word processing, spreadsheets, presentation graphics, etc.

Pioneered by office automation

The first widely usable basis for the concept of all-embracing object technology was supplied, not surprisingly, by Bill Gates' specialists at Microsoft, with COM and OLE, under the Windows umbrella.

And then there was OLE

Over the last ten years or so, the market has increasingly channeled all its energies towards specific concrete goals, and in the process the available language compilers have split up more and more into special-purpose tools. But with COM and OLE, the focal point of activities has shifted, almost imperceptibly, and this technology has matured into a *de facto* standard. One side-effect, incidentally, is that the development team now responsible for Windows must be one of the world's largest concentrations of acknowledged authorities on object technology.

Gurus by the score

Other vendors are adopting similar approaches, with differing rigor and, as we shall see, with differing priorities. Some 350 vendors and software companies around the world have combined to form the Object Management Group (OMG). Its aim is to standardize object-oriented methodology, irrespective of applications, and also of computer and operating system distinctions. The grouping includes Microsoft, along with DEC and IBM.

Many roads lead to object technology

CAD/CAM software, a late developer?

So products that demonstrate the technology's direct benefits to the user are now already available in various fields – but not in the technical software market.

Entirely excusable

There are of course reasons why CAD/CAM/CAE systems got on board relatively late and are only now beginning to develop suitable platforms and products:

Don't run before you can walk

1. The functionality of these systems is highly complex. It has taken a long time for them to be able to meet at least a reasonable proportion of their users' demands. So it will doubtless be obvious that one of the most difficult areas should not be the first place to choose when implementing a technological revolution of the magnitude of the shift to modern object technology.

Not really a job for niche-market specialists

2. Specialization among systems is very similar to specialization among departments in industrial product development, for example, and often corresponds to it directly. Just as business process re-engineering – gearing development to products and processes – cannot come from within a single department, it was equally unlikely that makers of specialized software would provide the general solution to the problem of integration.

Who is in charge?

The way things worked in practice – viewed impartially and in a good light – was (and is) frightening. In the energy industry, for example, users have their own specific requirements, which could have been met far more satisfactorily even with the resources of traditional CAD systems; but the people who directly influenced software development were in the surveying departments or external offices. Likewise, a mechanical package could easily have supplied the platform for unified, enterprise-wide use of parts lists, if only the walls between the commercial and technical sides were not so high. And in architecture, more satisfactory solutions could easily be conceived, except that every approach to development is based not on the needs of the majority of users (who here even more than elsewhere are split up among tiny engineering firms) but on the overall architectural plan.

But to be fair, even in business departments, which have had access to OLE-capable software since 1993, awareness of its full potential is probably limited to quite a small proportion of users. Its features are used as long as they are self-explanatory. Any additional benefits that might be drawn from it entail at the very least getting to grips with an unknown subject. And old dogs have a well-known aversion to learning new tricks. How many people have actually experimented with the OLE compound document facility when creating a lengthy document? I for one tried it out for the first time when writing this book, and I failed to find anyone who was able to give me advice based on personal experience.

Greater benefits call for personal initiative

Examples like this from the "simpler" environment of everyday office life also give some clue as to the potential efficiency for technical applications. There can be no doubt that the market needs this efficiency. From the user's viewpoint, object technology is the answer to the most urgent issue of recent years: the search for the tools best suited to supporting parallel working – concurrent engineering, as it is known in the field of industrial product development – among the greatest possible number of participating groups, whether or not they are on the same site, in the same country or even on the same continent, and above all regardless of the many different applications they are using.

Eminently suitable

Even in the medium term, the only way to satisfy industry's enormous demand for integrated and integration tools is to apply the methods of modern object technology.

Comprehensive integration

The show is on the road

The mechanism is there and the demand has long been there. Now it is up to the producers of standard software to adapt to this new situation quickly and effectively and draw the right conclusions. The way ahead is clear:

No room for monoliths now

No more monolithic monster systems; no more proprietary, standalone solutions. The demand now is for many small, flexible and fast components that can be used in combination and are perfectly adaptable with little effort to the needs of any workplace.

To gain a fuller appreciation of the scale of the changes facing us, we will now take a closer look at the nature of objects and venture deeper into the theory behind the technology that underlies them.

1.2 Basic Concepts

What's it all about?

These days, just about everyone (in the software sector, anyway) seems to be talking about object-oriented programming and object-oriented systems. All the more reason, then, to begin with a few fundamental observations on the topic. If you are interested enough to take a closer look, you will find that the same name is being used for some very different things. So first let's take the obvious question: what is an object?

Item with attitude

The object as the smallest element of an object-oriented system is an entity which incorporates its own description and knowledge of the methods by which it can be used. To put it another way, an object comprises the data which defines its properties and the functions that allow these properties to be put to work.

Print to file?

As an illustration, consider the MS-Windows Print Manager. This is an object which embodies all the conceivable properties needed to output documents. It knows about fonts, printers, the drivers that are needed, and also the applications that are used to create documents.

At the same time the Print Manager object offers users a series of methods which allow them to select, configure and activate a suitable output device.

Thus the Print Manager is comparable with the actual printer that stands next to your computer. That, too, possesses the properties needed to print on paper (such as color cartridge, paper-feed mechanism or output tray) and at the same time provides various methods (buttons, keys, switches) for initiating printing. *Just like real life*

Hence the key to the definition is abstraction from physical forms and concentration on the significant properties and ways of behaving which differentiate one object from another. *Abstract entity*

One object does not make a system. For many objects to work together meaningfully in a common environment, rules for their coexistence must be defined, and there should be laws governing certain principles of interaction between objects. *In perfect harmony*

What characterizes objects?

Over the years, terminology has become standardized, and the following terms are now used to describe the central attributes of object-oriented systems: *Essentials*

1. An **object** is a self-contained entity consisting of properties (data) and behavior (described by functions).
2. **Methods** describe the behavior of the object and provide for interaction between objects on the basis of a defined exchange of information (or messages).
3. Objects with similar properties and methods form **classes**, which are arranged hierarchically.
4. Within class hierarchies there is the possibility of **inheritance** of properties and methods.

The major benefits of this technology are now widely known. Reuse of existing objects clearly belongs at the top of the list. It minimizes the effort required to define new and modify old functionalities and properties of a system. That allows software to be more compact and easier to maintain, extend and adapt. *Recurring objects*

Classmates   Let's stay with the example of the printer. All the properties which essentially relate to the output of data are common to all output devices, be they laser printers, fax machines or plotters, so they do not need to be defined afresh each time. Instead, all output devices are assigned to a class of similar objects.

From birth   The simplest form of organization for such object classes is inheritance in a fixed hierarchy. A plotter is then simply defined as a member of the output device class and is automatically given all the properties typical of that class.

The danger with objects

Trouble with   Unfortunately, the initial euphoria over this great advan-
the relations   tage soon waned. For the more complex the systems became, the more the very reason for this advantage proved to be a barely surmountable obstacle. The problem was that, with more complex applications, the various types of inheritance that were initially adopted led right back to barely manageable dependency relationships.

1.3 Problems with Inheritance

Only looks simple   The first inheritance theory for objects is *simple implicit inheritance*, where properties are transmitted automatically. It works on the assumption that there is just one base class from which all subsequent classes, subclasses and objects take their definition. However, a situation which is still clear and comprehensible when there are few objects or few classes grows ever more involved and complex as the scale of the system increases.

Widespread,   The second form, *multiple implicit inheritance*, is borrowed directly from Mendelian genetics, the science which studies how parental characteristics are transmitted to the

Implicit Inheritance

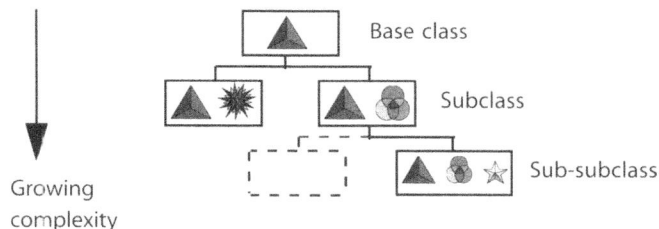

Figure 4: "This simple method is only capable of mapping simple relationships."

next generation in plants, animals and man. *Multiple implicit inheritance* is used in almost all object-oriented programming languages.

It is far more complicated than simple implicit inheritance, since here the base configuration consists of two or more base classes (parents). Allowing for all the conceivable combinations – including "incest" or "bigamy" – this model is scarcely capable of mapping even "parent-child relationships" reliably over a slightly longer chain of "generations".

but unreliable

Multiple Implicit (Mendelian) Inheritance

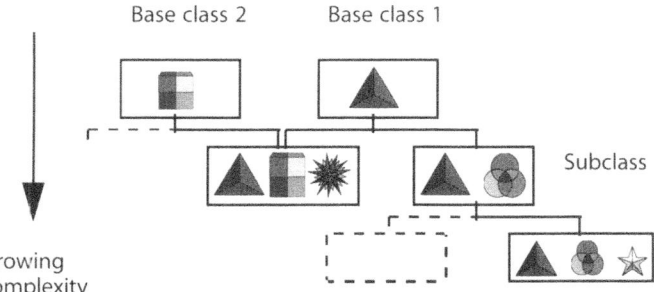

Figure 5: "Even with only two base classes, by the second or third generation it is already unclear which properties are transmitted. This model of inheritance likewise does not offer a sensible approach for more complicated relationships, such as apply in graphical data processing."

Defined, but unclear relationships

Allocation required

Consequently, there is a third method which does not involve automatic transmission of "hereditary characteristics". In this case, whenever an object is created, it is necessary to specify explicitly which properties from which classes will be transmitted to the new object. This *explicit inheritance* mechanism allows for ordered complexity, and it is increasingly the method of choice in object-oriented systems.

Ideal but not realistic

While this method does offer a solution to the handling of growing complexity, this form of inheritance only regulates one-way dependencies. In other words, like the previous methods it assumes that there are fixed relationships, that in each case there are indisputable relations between objects.

If this restriction is unacceptable, we are at a loss for a suitable method. A glance at any CAD application, to say nothing of the 3D modeling applications which are rapidly

Explicit Inheritance

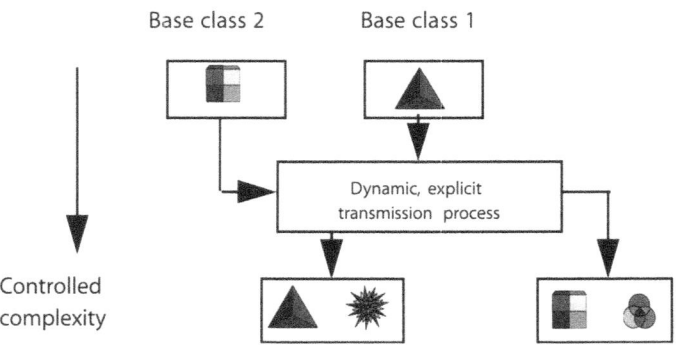

Figure 6: "The diagram shows that even this mechanism, while quite capable of managing more complex relationships, still only describes one-way, fixed relationships, which are not often encountered in real life."

becoming standard, immediately makes it clear that this is definitely not the place to be talking of low complexity and easily comprehensible relationships.

Hunt the father

O n the contrary: the genesis of a design and of components and discrete elements of it, the geometrical and non-geometrical dependencies among them, the *constraints* – all these things are of such great importance here that in recent times many systems have been hugely successful not least because they provide optimum service in precisely this area. And these relationships are by no means always fixed and clear. We repeatedly encounter reciprocal influences which cannot be described by inheritance alone.

Inheritance is no guarantee

The COM concept in its original form essentially does not involve inheritance of properties and manages entirely without this criterion of object-oriented systems. In terms of the office automation environment that is no great loss. An object is created once, and it notes its defined origin (the associated application), the place where it is stored, and the place where it is inserted. That is all that is required. The only sense in which the object has a link to other objects is that it may be a copy of an existing element.

Modest but effective

We conclude: object technology may solve many of the problems that have long plagued CAD developers and users; but if it is not capable of managing fixed relationships between parts and highly complex assemblies, as it stands it is unacceptable for CAD/CAM/CAE applications for that reason alone. Thus the resolving of this paradox demands maximum priority.

Wanted: objects with good relations

We shall see how this obstacle is cleared away by future Windows versions and by the extensions to the OLE concept for technical applications that are the subject of this book.

1.4 Object-Oriented or Object-Based?

Abstract solution

The Object Management Group (OMG), already mentioned above, has initially responded to the evident problem of implementing object properties by framing its fundamental definitions of unified object technology without a clear specification of how it should be achieved. The group aims at the greatest possible unity, so standardization has to operate at a very high level of abstraction, a level far enough from the practical needs of individual applications.

Differential propagation

In Object Management Architecture (OMA), anyway, the term *subtyping* is used instead of inheritance. Here, subtypes are the descendants of types, which are OMA's equivalent of object classes. There is no indication of the exact line of descent. That is left up to the individual system.

Thus the problem of relationships that we looked at in the previous section, particularly in terms of the lack of explicitness, is not resolved but simply put to one side.

A broker for objects

The heart of the OMG specifications on machine-independent object system architectures is the *object request broker (ORB)*. The way this governs communication between objects is defined in specifications which go by the name of the *Common Object Request Broker Architecture (CORBA)*.

Competition

These specifications are the immediate basis for the product which is in competition with OLE – OpenDoc. This aims to provide UNIX, the PowerPC and other platforms with services similar to OLE on PCs. It may well be able to support satisfactory solutions on heterogeneous networks sooner than OLE, but its chances of cornering the market appear to be shrinking. The Dataquest study quoted earlier predicts that Apple operating systems, currently with a market share of around 10 percent, will drop back to under 5 percent over the next five years.

Restricted communications

The advantage of the CORBA architecture for heterogeneous networks is offset by the disadvantage that it does not allow concurrent applications to intercommunicate in the same way as OLE. We shall now examine the OLE approach in more detail.

If we observe the terminological rules which have evolved over long years, a system which does not feature a defined sequence of inheritance – the fourth attribute of object-oriented systems – is strictly speaking not *object-oriented*, but merely a *class-based* system. If it does not have classes either, omitting the third main attribute as well, it is actually just *object-based*.

Strictly speaking class-based

From today's point of view it is quite likely that distinctions like these will in the long term weaken and lose their significance; yet we should not totally lose sight of the basic differences.

Thus if we stick to the conventional terminology, OLE is essentially a class-based mechanism, not object-oriented, because barring individual exceptions there is no transmission of characteristics, either by objects or by classes.

Barring exceptions, no inheritors

One exception relates to three properties which all COM object interfaces inherit from the *IUnknown* interface: *QueryInterface*, *AddRef* and *Release*. (This topic is dealt with in rather more detail in section 2.2.) The other exception is the method of *aggregation*, which under certain conditions allows properties of various source objects to be combined to form new properties in a new object. Externally this changes nothing about the appearance of the object, as the aggregated properties are made available in exactly the same way as the original object properties.

Sneak preview

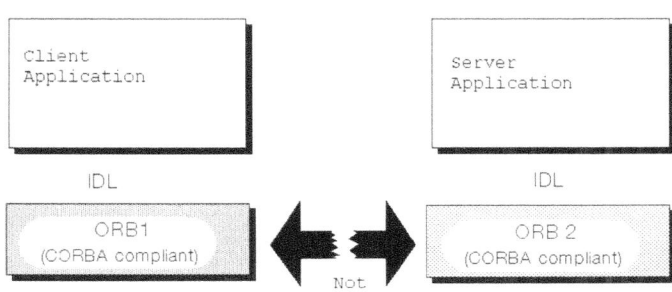

Figure 7: "The interoperability problem has not yet been solved in the CORBA concept." (Figure 4.4 from Meyer/Obermayr, "Objekte integrieren mit OLE 2")

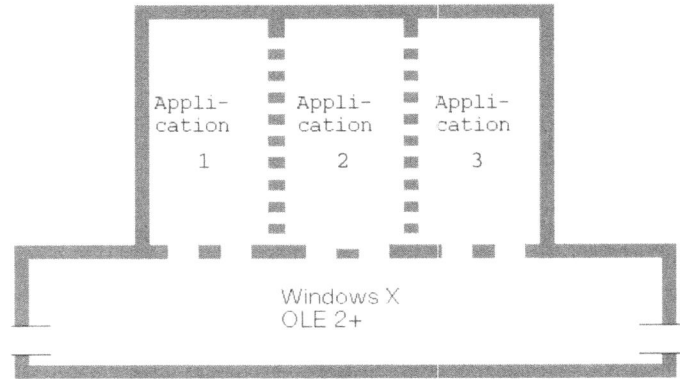

Figure 8: "Communication between different applications is the focal point of the OLE/COM mechanism." (Figure 3.9 from Meyer/Obermayr)

No harm done　　For users of what were previously the most important OLE applications, concentrating on the creation of multimedia documents and simple databases, the lack of inheritance is really only a minor blemish. The resultant benefit, interoperability, takes precedence.

All for the best　　This advantage of OLE, compared to other OMA concepts for example, is in fact hugely beneficial to users: it allows them to work with applications of widely varying origin, regardless of the source code and hence of the programming language in which it is written. By contrast, all known mechanisms which feature inheritance are extremely restricted in the extent to which they can be language independent.

Object technology in the operating system　　The operating system itself, which receives the various programming languages and data structures of applications translated into its machine language, must be the bond that allows objects to intercommunicate. Object technology must be the nucleus of a standardized operating system. That is the approach adopted for Windows NT and Windows 95.

The concern that reliance on OLE/COM, i.e. Microsoft Windows, may result in greater problems when concurrently using CORBA applications cannot simply be dismissed, since it is not yet possible to perform suitable tests owing to the unavailability of software.

Yet there are many signs that this hitch will quite soon be sorted out to mutual benefit. After all, it is in the OpenDoc community's best interests to understand OLE objects and make them usable in the OpenDoc environment – and vice versa. In addition to which, Microsoft is working together with DEC on the next version of the COM mechanism, which is intended to match up with the CORBA specifications in all major respects.

Convergence

Platform for Integration

Ms-Windows and OLE:

2

2 MS-Windows and OLE: Platform for Integration

When the first versions of MS-Windows were released some years ago, there were some – PC novices – who were happy that it was now (almost) unnecessary to know anything about the operating system. Others – experienced DOS users or those with Macintoshes – smiled sympathetically. It wasn't a bad start, but it was so slow and awkward and above all prone to frequent crashes that widespread use was slow to take off.

Hesitant takeoff

That the situation is now entirely different is not only due to the fact that PCs are nowadays faster, cheaper and generally equipped with MS-Windows from the start. It has as much if not more to do with the robustness, ease of use and effectiveness that the graphic user interface now offers.

Effective and fairly stable

The major influence behind this rise in the fortunes of MS-Windows is doubtless the OLE mechanism, even if users are mostly unaware of it.

The reason is very simple: OLE is geared to the interests of users and at the same time offers a unified, open concept to all application writers as a mechanism for integrating their products.

Open to all

2.1 The OLE/COM Mechanism

OLE was created with the primary aim of improving integration between documents from different applications. Creating a *link* between a word processing document and a graphic produced by another application or

Document mix

First there is the compound document

Objects with a pedigree

embedding a spreadsheet into a presentation were features that were already available in Version 1 of OLE.

The starting point for the whole process is the primary document which is being created or modified by the user. This is known as the *compound document* if it incorporates other objects. One example might be a press release with a table of sales figures built into it. Other objects which are far easier to edit with special applications, such as a spreadsheet, a presentation graphic or a database, can be inserted in the compound document without the need to quit the primary application.

Compared to conventional methods of converting full or partial copies of files and placing them in a suitable position, OLE offers considerable advantages. No copying of a file is involved. Instead, you are inserting an object which is aware of its relationship to its source. Thus there is no need to translate from one data structure to another.

The two ways of inserting objects differ in the form of their relationship with their source.

The Origins of OLE:
Integrating Data from Other Applications

Linked spreadsheet

The graphic is automatically updated from the spread-sheet

Graphic with link to spreadsheet

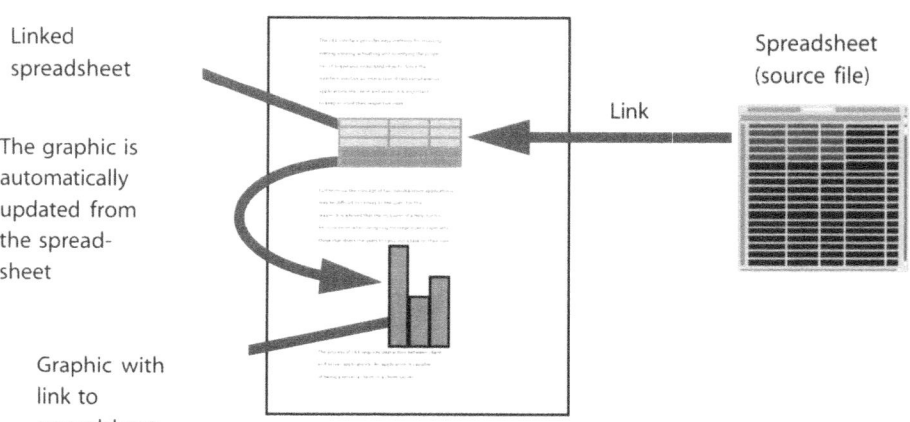

Spreadsheet (source file)

Link

Figure 9: "A typical example. Data from a spreadsheet is incorporated in a text document. The graphic derived from this data is not created using word processor resources, either. Under Windows, these actions do not call for any conversion work."

Linking

I f an object is pasted in as a *link*, no copying is involved. Instead, the link defines a reference to an external file. Only the reference is placed within the compound document; the object itself remains external. The same applies even if it is only selected data that is being treated as an object.

Good references

In this case all changes to the linked object are necessarily changes to the original; and every time a change is made to the original, the same change will be reproduced in all the documents that include a link to it.

There is only one

OLE allows you to destroy this *link* later and *embed* the object instead.

Flexible

Embedding

W hen an object is *embedded*, i.e. inserted without linking, from that point on it is an original component of the compound document. The connection between the copy and the original object is broken, and changes to the source do not affect the embedded element.

Separate copy

Nevertheless we are dealing with objects here – the embedded item retains its internal data structure and does not need to be converted. It also continues to remember which application was used to create it, and that the application remains responsible for the object and for making any modifications to it.

Good memory

Creating

P erhaps a different instance of object integration occurs more often: the object does not yet exist at the time it is needed. That changes practically nothing about

Be creative

the procedure we have just described. In this case the required object is either created as the original object, and a copy is linked to the compound document, or it is placed in the primary file as the original with no reference to any external element.

In-place activation

Always on the ball

*I*n-place activation (or *in-place editing*) in OLE terms refers to the editing of objects using the original application when the object is in a "foreign" environment.

Quick-change This feature is very handy for the user. To modify an *artist* object there is now no need to switch applications or

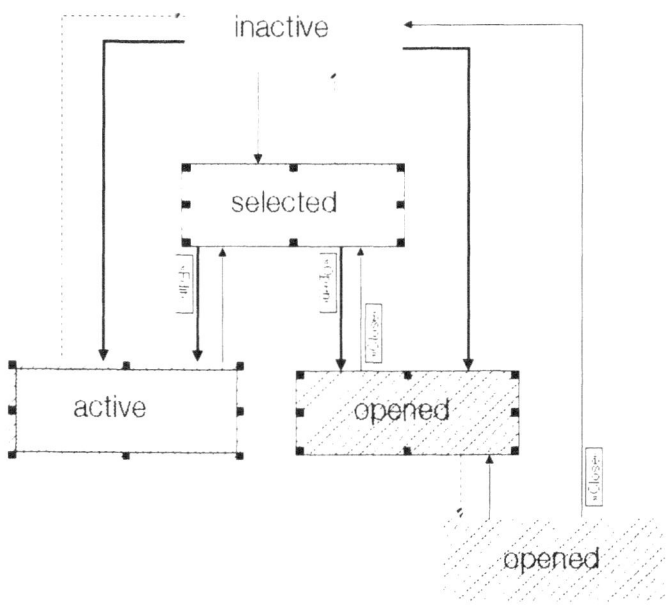

Figure 10: "This diagram illustrates the various states of objects and the dependence on mouse actions. When the object is 'activated' or 'opened', basically all that changes is the menu." (Figure 5-12, Meyer/Obermayr)

open an extra window. Instead, as you edit the compound document, the applications are activated as and when you need them. The process looks something like this:

1. The main menu bar typically remains unchanged, though there may be extra functions on individual menus such as *File* or *Help*.

    Standard menus

2. The actual window in which the compound document together with its linked or embedded objects is displayed and edited likewise remains almost identical. Its size may be slightly reduced from the top down owing to the addition of extra menu bars.

    On permanent display

3. In one or more extra menu bars the application invoked for *in-place editing* now supplies exactly those functions that you need in order to modify the current object.

    Everything else you need

Externally and in terms of operation, the procedure is no different from switching between different areas of a single application. If you switch from ordinary word processing to the mail merge facility, you follow the same procedure as a user editing a chart within a compound document.

It all takes place in response to a double click, so quickly and unobtrusively and without further action on the part of the user that surveys on experienced and inexperienced PC users alike have shown that in many cases people failed to notice that a foreign application had been activated, or only noticed with some surprise after a considerable delay.[1]

Almost without noticing

[1] *Objekte integrieren mit OLE 2, Meyer/ Obermayr*

Thus *in-place activation* gives the end user the impression of being within a single application environment with all the actions needed to create a complex document. This concept makes a reality of something that many have long been waiting for.

True utopia

2.2 The Component Object Model

Component nucleus

Now that we have sketched out the nature of the compound document as the goal of working with OLE, let us turn in rather more detail to the real nucleus of the mechanism, the type of object at the heart of all OLE developments. This type is known as the *Component Object Model*, abbreviated to *COM*. What is so special about *COM*, and why indeed was it necessary to define a special object type?

Each to his or her own?

As with any other software technology there are all kinds of approaches to object-oriented software, and they are by no means mutually compatible. On the contrary: the systems which have reached the market to date are all no different in this respect from earlier applications. Each has its own object type and its own style of message passing between objects.

Proprietary object technology

Thus even the systems that Intergraph itself has launched, I/EMS (for mechanical design) and TIGRIS/DYNAMO (for GIS), while being object-oriented systems, are nonetheless wholly proprietary. Each is based on a different approach to object technology, and both are no more compatible with other software products than any other system.

Standardization required

So if a comprehensive solution is really to be found, it is essential to define standards open to all for application designers to follow.

COM rules, OK?

Thus within the Microsoft Windows world a specification has been drafted to form a standard of this type, and at the heart of this specification there is the *Component Object Model*, which tells all developers in minute detail how any object that wants to be part of this world must be constructed.

Encapsulation

The first principle of *COM* is one that it shares with every other object-oriented system: *encapsulation*. The object and its properties, i.e. data, are shielded from the outside world and protected against access. Nobody is allowed to modify the data; only the object itself is allowed to do so.

Keep it under cover

To edit a spreadsheet built into a presentation graphic you cannot use the functionality of the presentation software itself. To make changes to anything other than its position or size you have to activate the spreadsheet program. Unless, that is, it is possible to convert the object to the format of the presentation graphic, in which case it ceases to exist as an object and incorporates its data into the larger object formed by the graphic.

Indirect access

To allow this approach to be open to all suitably equipped applications, the COM mechanism includes a further level of abstraction. The behavior of the object is implemented in the form of methods which are made available to the environment. The COM specification describes how this is to be regulated, and that is by means of *interfaces*. Similar

Unknown quantity

Object Technology

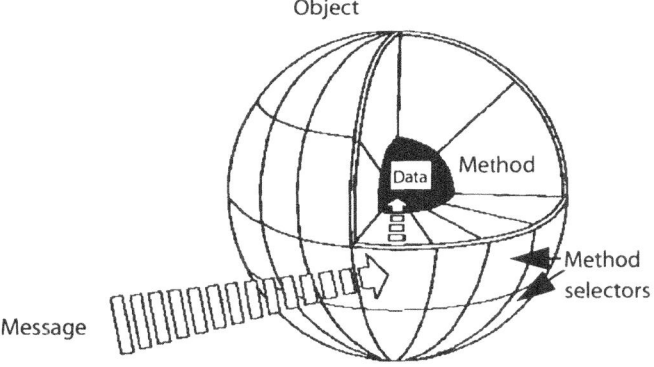

Figure 11: "In general terms you can visualize object encapsulation like this. The properties and the behavior are protected. The only contact is in the form of message passing." (Figure 1 from Dr. Oesterhelt's speech in 1990)

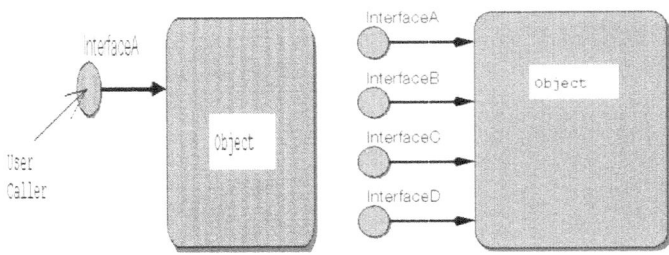

Figure 12: "As a user you have no direct access to a COM object. To use its functionality you have to go via its interfaces." (Figures 7-16 and 7-17, Meyer/Obermayr)

methods are grouped in interfaces. This is all done in such a way that no object (and no developer or user) needs to know how the individual object and its methods are implemented.

Point to it

An interface in this context is nothing more than a group of pointers to the methods of the object. Thus to trigger a method an outside object needs to know which interface contains the pointer to that method.

Central switchboard:
Query-
Interface

So how do you find out the right interfaces and the pointers they contain? Simple: by trying them out. However, since that would not only take too long but would result in a multitude of futile calls to objects, there is a central element known as the *QueryInterface* which must be present in every OLE object.

Do you know this one?

And now communication is quite easy. If Object A knows about a single interface of Object B, it can talk to the *QueryInterface* to ask about another one. Not about all those that are available in B, but about a specific one that interests A.

You have to be smart

Now we have killed two birds with one stone. You cannot call B unless you know of at least one interface; but if you can get to B, you are certain of being able to access the other interfaces and hence the object's methods using selective queries.

Highly versatile

It's like getting to know someone. What language does the other person speak? (Which interfaces are supported?) How do I communicate with that person, and what can they do for me? (What are the methods behind these interfaces?) Once that has been established, opinions can be

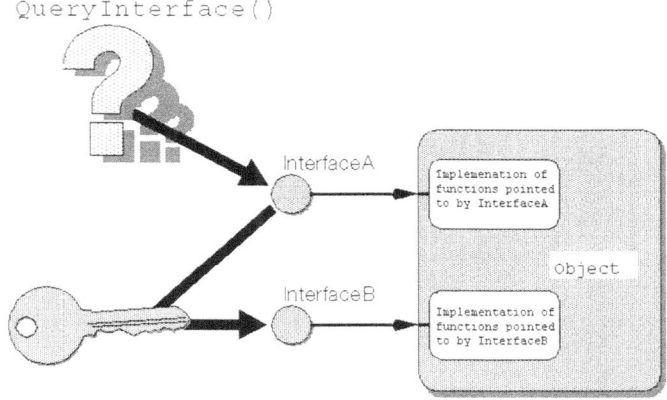

QueryInterface()

Figure 13: "This is how the user finds out whether the selected object offers the required function." (Figure 7-22, Meyer/Obermayr)

exchanged, and requests can be made, rejected or accepted. Just as every person will react differently to a remark by a particular speaker, every object has its own highly individual way of responding to information. Among objects this form of behavior is known as *polymorphism*.

Self-counter

In addition to *QueryInterface* there are two other elements that are encountered in every COM object – one function (called *AddRef*) which increments a counter by one each time the object is accessed, and another (called *Release*) which turns the counter back by one each time an access is completed.

Ups and downs

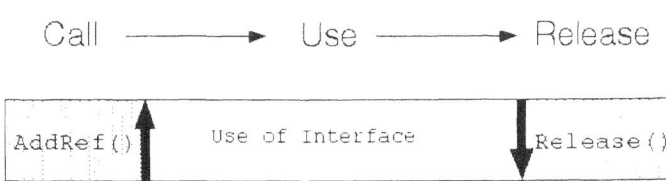

Figure 14: "Use of a COM object is subject to strict rules." (Figure 7-24, Meyer/Obermayr)

*Relatively
independent*

Thus each object is truly its own master. It knows when it is being used. It can be loaded, invoked, activated and sent information by a number of different objects at the same time. It also notices when there are no other objects using it and puts itself to sleep or terminates its existence as an object.

2.3 The Benefits of OLE

Allocating roles

To enable component objects from disparate applications to be used together, Microsoft has created an environment in which certain things are regulated on a binding basis with a view to enhancing ease of use: the roles of the applications, and mechanisms for finding, exchanging, moving and representing objects.

2.3.1 Client and Server

Rights and duties

Any form of coexistence entails certain agreements on who has what rights and how the roles of the individuals are shared out in the community. This occurs even in the smallest community where the relationship is only between two people. There are fixed rules which it may be punishable to transgress. Conversely, there are also rules on a much more flexible level which are to some extent self-regulating and are subject to constant alteration.

*Communication is
vital*

Since with modern object technology we are attempting to reflect real life and the real world, it is evident that similar arrangements to those that apply in society should have their equivalents in an object-oriented mechanism like OLE. Their purpose is to simplify and speed up interaction between objects and hence of course between the user and the software – and at the same time make it stable and secure.

The roles that an application, i.e. a programmed object, can play within OLE are clearly defined. Anyone designing OLE-compliant components must observe these conventions and decide where a new object is to fit into the OLE community. The main question to resolve concerns the side an object is to stand on in the relationship between compound document and insertion, between the container and the contained.

Guidelines for developers

The compound document is said to be a *client*, acting as a *container* for any other objects. The objects it contains are said to be provided by a *server*. This is terminology we know from the field of computer networking, but here it is merely used by analogy and essentially has nothing to do with an object's presence or position on a network.

Another kind of client/ server architecture

As in real life, the roles of *client* and *server*, customer and service provider, may be highly complex and also change constantly – though of course they must have

And/or or exclusively

OLE-Style Client and Server

Here the word processor is the client and the spreadsheet program is the server (relative to the objects 'Spreadsheet' and 'Graphic')

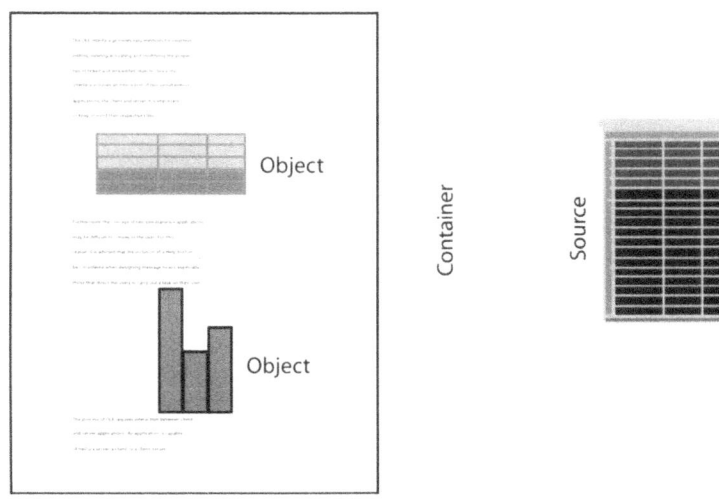

Figure 15: "Clear separation between object user and provider"

been designed to do so by their creator. The following properties and combinations of them are defined within OLE:

1. The *pure container* holds linked and embedded objects but does not itself make objects available to other applications for linking or embedding.
2. The *link container* is capable of inserting and linking objects, and it makes objects of its own available for linking.
3. The *simple object application* exclusively provides objects for embedding and linking, and that means only objects which have to be linked or embedded in their entirety.
4. The *pseudo object application* is likewise restricted to acting as an object provider, but on request it will also supply parts of objects.
5. The *link object application* acts exclusively as a source of objects which may be linked but not embedded.
6. Last there is the *container and object application*, which is a kind of super-being in OLE. It can hold linked and embedded objects, but where required it can also provide objects for linking and embedding.

Intentional restrictions, selective service

For users, these distinctions are of some significance. If you fail to observe them when first getting to grips with OLE technology, you may well be surprised to find that not every object will do the same thing in every place. Bitter experience from other fields may lead you to think you have come upon yet another programming error or some weakness in the system, but it is actually the way OLE is designed to work: not every object is intended to be able to do everything. Furthermore, applications are not all intended to have the same ranking and the same sphere of influence. This simplifies interaction between applications as well as application programming, and in the final analysis it also makes the systems themselves easier to use.

2.3.2 OLE Automation

On the basis of what you have read so far, you will probably have guessed how this allocation of roles is regulated. Correct: like all the others, these properties of an application can only be queried and activated by way of their interfaces. Thus for each of the defined object classes there are special interfaces which provide access to the functionality of the objects and allocate an object to a particular role.

Once more: interfaces control everything

In the OLE world this message-passing mechanism is known as *automation*. It specifies how an object should *expose* its methods and offer them as a *service* to other objects and how this service should be accessed by the *client*. The only way to exchange anything other than messages is to send the *"Data Transfer"* message, and this action naturally entails establishing the language in which such an extensive communication is to take place.

Display your goods and offer a service

OLE Automation

The client accesses objects by means of automation

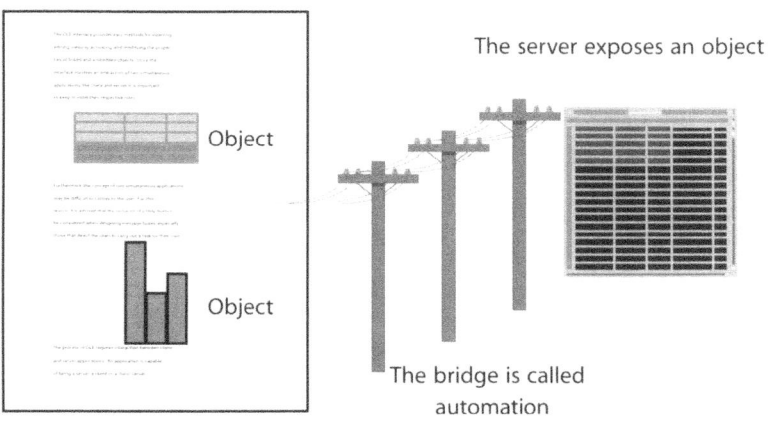

Figure 16: "OLE automation is the bridge that lets messages pass between client and server."

Like a real object

One special feature of automation is the use of what are known as *pseudo-objects.* A pseudo-object is created when a container links part of an object (a number of cells from a spreadsheet, for example). The link is then made using a precise identifier for the object, known as the *item moniker*, the moniker being the name of the structure of the linked partial object as used to address it within the container.

Connection for concurrent operation

Disparate application programs which support OLE automation are able to work together without needing to know any details of each other's characteristics, functions or structures. They simply need information about the objects and messages that are available.

Only the essentials

Another aspect of this is that for purposes of in-place activation there is no need to implement the full functionality of an application. It is enough to supply just those menu items that are required to perform the desired action.

To jump ahead a little, this naturally also applies to applications which were written using traditional methods and have been made OLE-capable, a topic dealt with in section 4.3. In this case the adaptation work can be reduced to a minimum and its scope is easier to estimate.

2.3.3 Data Exchange

The dynamics of data exchange

Initial experiences of exchanging data dynamically between disparate applications date from the pre-OLE era, and in the Microsoft annals they go by the name of DDE (Dynamic Data Exchange). These experiences have left their mark on the mechanism for exchanging object data in differing formats which is now used in OLE. The technical term for this mechanism is *uniform data transfer*. This new method has completely superseded DDE.

Regardless of data structure

Uniform data transfer typically allows presentation and text data in different formats to be merged in a compound document. Any actions intended to transfer objects between different applications and objects utilize this side of OLE.

It is up to application developers to decide which format their applications are to use to transfer data and which formats they are to be able to understand and process. In the worst-case scenario that may be restricted to the application's own language, its *native format*, which may be proprietary; but it may include many native formats; or following agreement between software vendors it may incorporate one or more generally used standard formats.

From mother tongue to standard dialect

2.3.4 Drag-and-Drop Editing

This is probably the OLE functionality that has so far attracted the most admirers. And it was the first to allow Windows to present itself to the PC user as a system which calls for nothing but intuition, demanding no hard-won expertise or complicated menu operations.

Intuitive

Drag – you select an object, a word, a worksheet or a graphic with the mouse and shift it to another position by moving the mouse with the button held down.

The event controls the software ...

Drop – you release the mouse button, and the object comes to rest at its new location.

Event-driven repositioning of parts of documents existed before Windows and OLE, but it worked only within a single application and with very simple objects. Now the technique extends to moving objects between totally different and foreign applications – provided, of course, that they support OLE and drag-and-drop.

.. across application boundaries

Like drag-and-drop, *Copy* and *Paste* can be used across application boundaries under OLE, and the user no longer notices temporary storage in a buffer, as that now happens automatically in the background.

Functionality like this would not be possible without the underlying Component Object Model and the specifications governing the creation of standardized representations of different objects. Under traditional conditions the functions and the data would be separate. Moving any object would result in a trailing string of database operations required to

Praise be to COM

guarantee that the object was fully and correctly described at its new location.

2.3.5 Files and Structured Storage

Storage: what, where and how

Having got the functionality sorted out, we now need to deal with the data structures. These, too, have to be suitably organized, in spite of all our talk of objects and encapsulation. Indeed, we need them precisely in order to implement objects and encapsulation. If the entire document is no longer to be converted and stored in the same format in a single file, we need to define new rules for storage.

Traditional storage and modern objects

In this respect OLE applications currently still suffer from a shortcoming, because it is necessary to know the exact path and file name of an object with a defined link in a container. In other words, COM objects are still managed within the framework of the storage system defined for conventional files.

Future perfect

In the pipeline there is a *structured storage* mechanism, based essentially on the new object technology and forming part of a comprehensive *object-oriented file system* or *OFS*. It will be available with the Cairo version of Windows.

"The superfile"

The data for all the objects contained in a compound document will then be collected and stored in a single file, known as the *compound file*.

Files within files

This principle aims to allow highly disparate data and data structures to be stored within a single file. In effect it is equivalent to having a directory structure or a file system inside a file.

Indeed, all the major components of a file system are to be encountered in the compound file model:

Stream

1. The equivalent of the file as the smallest unit on the hard disk is the *stream object*. This contains the object data proper. Its name is assigned by the application, not the user; and the form of the data, i.e. its internal structure, is

of no significance to the user or the application. The important thing for the application controlling the compound document, is simply to know which application is responsible for creating the data.

2. The equivalent of the *root directory* is the *root storage object*. This represents the actual file as a unit in the overall system, and its name is identical to the file name of the compound document.   *Root*

3. Just as the tree of directories (or folders), subdirectories and files branch off from the root directory on a hard disk, the compound file is subdivided into further *storage objects*, which may in turn contain stream objects and storage objects.   *Storage*

The difference between the form of storage that still prevails under Windows 3.1 and the future structured storage can best be illustrated with reference to an obvious example:

The book you are now reading was written as a compound document in Microsoft Word. All its chapters and   *This book, for example*

The Structured Storage Model

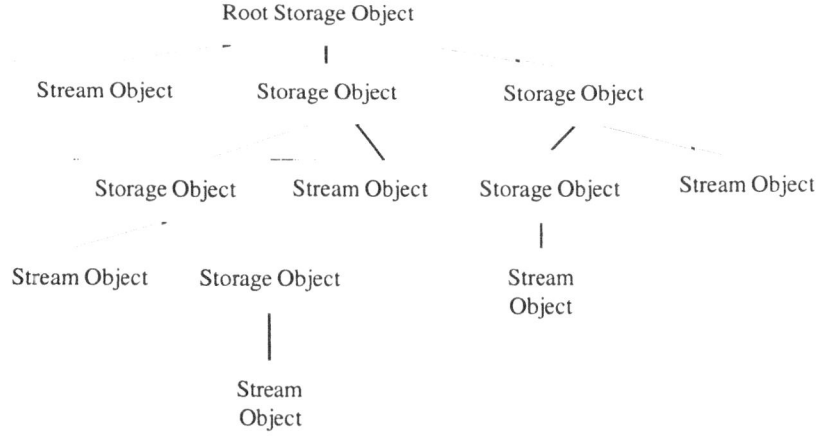

Figure 17: "The diagram shows the relationships between the elements of a future structured storage system."

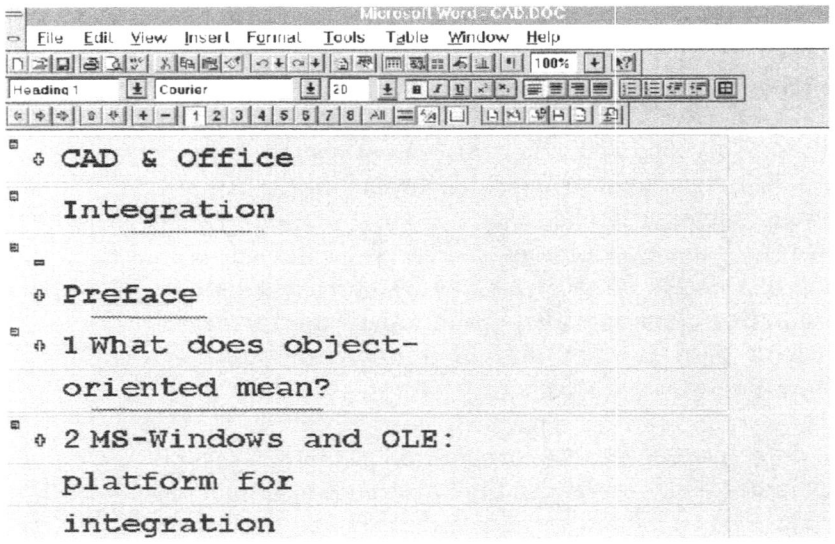

Figure 18: "In the master document, only the first level has been activated (using button 1 on the lowest toolbar). Consequently, only the main headings are displayed. Each sub-document has a thin frame around it, with an icon in the top left-hand corner which allows it to be edited directly."

sections exist as individual objects inserted as links in a container, the compound or master document. Thus the book can be opened in its entirety and displayed in various views – *Normal, Outline, Page Layout* or *Master Document* – even though it contains nothing but the links to the individual *sub-documents.*

Big benefits   That has brought huge advantages over earlier approaches. Continuous page numbering, for example, can be controlled automatically for all the chapters. You can press a button and have all the chapter and section headings printed out separately exactly as they would appear in the table of contents, because if you switch on only the first two or three *levels*, the body of the text will be hidden. The ability to switch rapidly between the master view and the normal editing view makes your work easier and drastically reduces the number of file-open activities – all you need to do is double-click on an icon in the master document. You can also use the master document for global text replacement or global reformatting. In short, the twin advantages of working on small units and of central document management are both brought to bear and are not mutually exclusive.

However, what happens when you copy the book to a floppy disk is this: First you have to store the master document, typically under *a:*. Then you have to edit all the individual documents again and store them in turn under *a:*. This transfers the *paths* of the objects. Finally, having done that, you have to remove the read-only lock which is applied by default to each document.

Temporary drawback

It's only then that the book can be further processed by the publisher. That is because all that the master document actually contains is the references to files and path names. Once the files are no longer on the same path, the entire management of the combined documents breaks down.

Nothing in it but references

By contrast, the structured storage principle will provide a way in which the user will only have to worry about the master document, while all the logical branches, links and dependencies of the objects should be handled by the operating system.

Solution in sight

We shall return to this data storage model later in conjunction with the design and modeling extensions to OLE, since it naturally plays a major part in relation to data security.

High priority

2.3.6 Monikers, Visual Basic and Other Benefits

Monikers

Thus OLE/COM offers a set of carefully designed mechanisms aimed at supporting interoperation between different applications. The main advantage – compared to other systems written in C++ or C, for example – is probably the fact that the underlying object

Interoperable from the start

The OLE/COM Concept

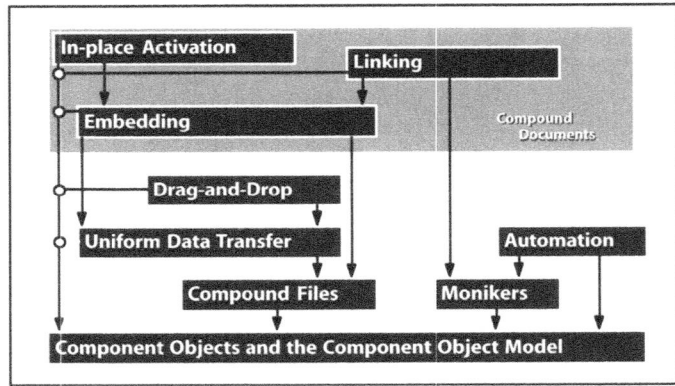

based on: Inside OLE 2 **by K. Brockschmidt**

Figure 19: "The entire OLE 2 environment looks like this, with all the major components and relationships included."

specifications were geared from the very beginning to message passing across process boundaries.

As in a single program   In conjunction with OLE/COM, objects from completely different applications can work together exactly as they can within a single application.

A related topic is that of *monikers.* The term refers to a unified procedure for finding objects and making them available to the user (or rather the container application).

High-speed search   A moniker is a unique identifier for an object, or for the place where the object is to be found. When a component is supplied by the server and linked or embedded by the client, a moniker is generated at the same time, containing precise details of what the object is called, where it is stored, and what size it is (or what part of the object is involved). These details are always unique to the object and are typically of the following form:

[2] Meyer/Obermayr:
Objekte integrieren
mit OLE 2, p. 99

Source: C:\FILES\OLE\TESTS\TAB:XLS\Z2S1:Z5S2[2]

Dynamic-Link Library

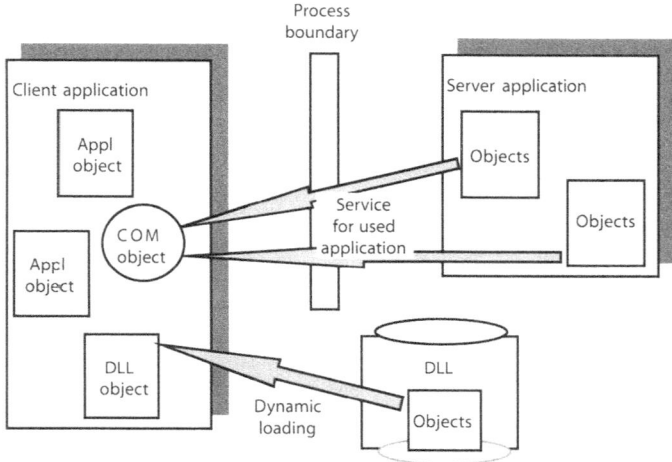

Figure 20: "The dynamic-link library, like any other server, provides the client with objects which are not loaded until the moment they need to be used."

Using libraries

As objects on this basis can be used any number of times, and because they are loaded in binary form and only at the moment they are needed for use, it was a logical step to set up a generally accessible library of standard objects for developers to call on when designing new software products.

The right object at the right time

Part of this library is a permanent component of Windows, in the form of a *dynamic-link library* (DLL). In addition there is a library, publicly accessible throughout the world, which already contains a few thousand objects and is growing steadily and ever more quickly.

Dynamic growth

Hence this object technology offers software development yet another major benefit: it does away with the need to keep developing new components for specific purposes when they already exist in the same or a similar form elsewhere. That makes it easier for developers to concentrate

No need to reinvent the wheel

on their own specialities, and also promotes the growing standardization of software technology. For there is an ever-growing number of functions of general significance which exist only once; their behavior is known, they are stable, and they have been thoroughly tested and debugged to a level which is scarcely achievable for a single application.

Global dialects

Esperanto?

Finally, there is one other point at which OLE technology goes further than previous object-oriented systems. All its components have been developed using the widely available programming tools *Visual Basic* and *Visual C++*. Furthermore, these tools are accessible to anyone for writing macros, extensions and their own developments – and at an almost negligible price level as well.

Programming's not just for wizards

So at last we are seeing the beginning of the end for the era in which users not only had to familiarize themselves with complicated menu structures, but were also forced to learn programming languages which were intricate and above all proprietary if they wanted to adapt applications to operational requirements in any way or add extra functions.

2.4 So Far, So Good

The "document" is not enough

Like all good things, of course, OLE/COM also has its downsides, or weak points rather. These have prevented the mechanism attaining greater significance outside the field of pure document creation.

Picture and computer graphic: not the same

In particular, the entire field of graphical data processing and of the CAD/CAM/CAE applications available

Figure 21: see Color Section

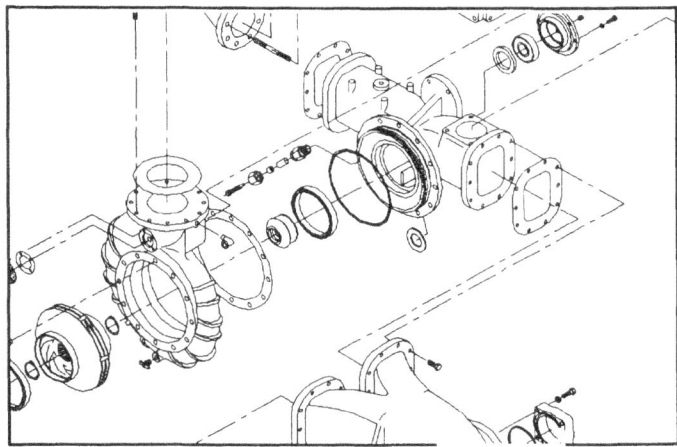

Figure 22: "Components can be shown, but can no longer be activated. This is a dead graphic with no dynamic reference to the original."

for it has been excluded from the benefits described in the previous section. When creating documentation it is generally sufficient to embed a "picture" and position it and to make sure that the text fits around it. Repositioning and resizing may also be required, and OLE provides for that, too. But that pretty much describes the full extent of the graphical world as it has been to date.

Restricted graphics

For users of CAD and GIS applications, perhaps wishing to integrate their data in a set of technical documentation, that was not enough. To say nothing of the more demanding requirements of the technical world.

Technical apps – another world

If you insert a map in a document, you lose all the information that was associated with the map in the GIS system. And that really means all of it, because even the relationships between the coordinates, the precisely defined ratio of longitude to latitude, are destroyed in the pixel image. The document knows nothing about coor-

A picture but no information

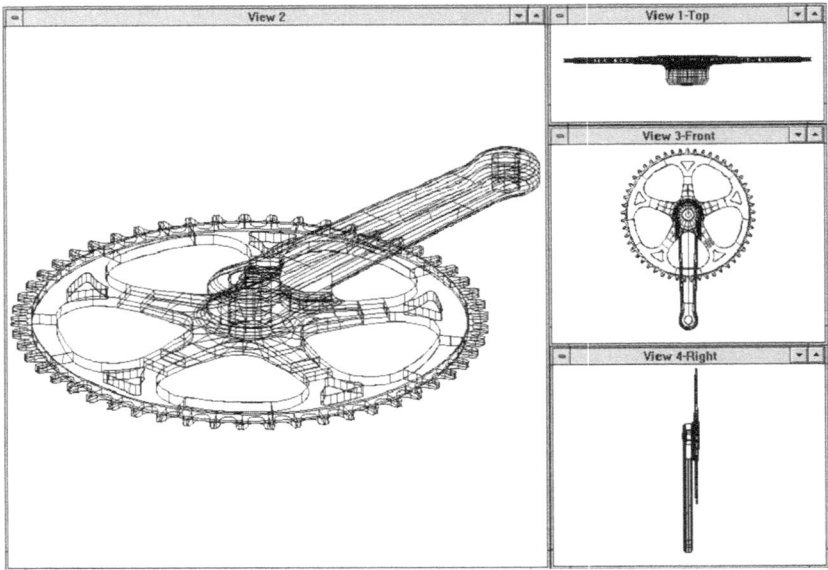

Figure 23 (see Color Section) and 24: "Incorporating mechanical components and then shading them and completely changing the way they are displayed – this is essential when dealing with CAD data, but it was not available under OLE 2."

dinates. At all costs you must avoid resizing the embedded object, as this will as a rule inevitably result in a change to the actual content of the graphic.

Largely useless The same naturally applies to 3D models in the field of mechanical design. You simply produce a 2D image of a model, and it loses all reference to its original properties. You cannot rotate it, for example, or join it to other elements.

The following list enumerates the primary limitations of OLE 2 with regard to CAD and related applications:

Rectangular 1. All objects by definition had a rectangular frame which had to fit on a single page. The size of the frame was largely independent of the geometry of the object itself.

Opaque 2. Objects were fundamentally not transparent and could not be superimposed. Instead, each object that was inserted replaced the element that was previously at the chosen location.

3. There were absolutely no specifications covering the definition of three-dimensional objects.

Flat

4. All the important properties of 2D and 3D elements relating to representation on the monitor or on other output devices were unknown to the OLE objects. That precluded the possibility of zooming, panning and rotation and of proportional scaling or shading – in fact all the visualization tools which are indispensable parts of CAD applications.

One-sided and inflexible

5. OLE was not designed to handle the extremely high volumes of data routinely encountered in 3D modeling and in graphical data processing in general.

Small-scale

6. Lastly, as discussed in the general introduction, OLE included no definition of the way to manage the relationships between elements and objects. There was no model of relationships suitable for use in CAD applications.

Unrelated

We are now familiar with the chief problems that had to be solved by anyone intending to use OLE as the basis for CAD systems for the future.

3 OLE for D&M

3 OLE for D&M

In 1993, when Intergraph committed itself to developing and offering all new software products under Windows or Windows NT, Version 2 of OLE had just hit the market. At that time not a single CAD vendor had made serious efforts to adapt the admirable principles inherent in OLE/COM technology to the requirements of graphical software applications.

Wide-open market

Microsoft itself is not a vendor of technical software, being more at home in the fields of office automation and operating systems. Hence support was the most that could be expected from that quarter, not an adequate technical solution, since the expertise was lacking.

Microsoft and CAD

So Intergraph was faced with the challenge of finding its own way to make OLE suitable for CAD, GIS and other graphical applications. With the hardware developers hard at work producing and marketing Technical Desktop PC workstations based on Windows and Windows NT, since the end of 1994 one of the world's largest software development teams has been devoting its energies to a project code-named *Jupiter* which has attracted a great deal of attention.

On course for Jupiter

In parallel with development work on new applications designed to make the advantages of object technology bring direct benefits to the end user, the specialists in Huntsville, Alabama, went about defining the extensions which were essential to ensuring the broader applicability of OLE technology.

Paving the way

These extensions basically involve additional OLE interfaces which serve to describe graphical 2D and 3D objects, to handle message passing between them, and to govern their location in the associated container application.

Three new groups of interfaces

Obviously it would have been possible to define these specifications without making them generally accessible. Intergraph could have defined a platform suitable for its

No half measures

Figure 25: "Mark Fortenberry is the man to turn to at Intergraph with questions about the OLE extensions."

own applications so as simply to make the benefits of OLE technology available to its own customers. Yet that would just have been another half measure.

No more proprietary solutions

Mark Fortenberry, manager of the development group responsible for OLE interfaces, puts it like this: "That would have been just one more proprietary solution. The time for software like that is now past. The true strength of OLE is the very fact that it allows totally different applications to operate together. If we want to extend its impact to the field of graphical applications, we have to formulate the primary interfaces in general terms and make them available to any developer who is interested."

Agreement with Microsoft and other vendors

At talks with Microsoft in May 1994, the project was discussed and the first practical examples were demonstrated. The OLE experts were fascinated. However, since this was a development originating from a single vendor, not the result of international standardization efforts, other leading CAE software houses were asked for feedback: Autodesk, SDRC, ANSYS and Spatial Technology were among the first to express an interest. By the end of 1994 there were enough positive signs to indicate that an initial concrete agreement could be reached.

Forming the club

At a joint meeting on January 24, 1995, it was agreed to adopt the defined interfaces as modified on the basis of consultation with the other vendors. The participants also agreed to set up a committee responsible for consolidating and propagating the new industry standard. This body is the *Design and Modeling Applications Council (DMAC)*.

Before very long, DMAC had been joined by numerous other companies, institutes and individuals, and a lively exchange of information and opinions was under way. The form that the discussions take is simplicity itself. An Internet address that anyone can access has been set up at Intergraph. The address is:

Communication on the net

OLECOUNCIL@INGR.COM

At this address any newcomer can get hold of the full specification of the interfaces that we will be discussing below; and every member automatically receives the full text of all the messages that have been exchanged between the interface developers and the other contributors to DMAC.

Anyone can listen in

At the time of writing, there are already over 40 registered members. They include Bentley Systems (MicroStation), Computervision (PELORUS), Dassault Systèmes (Catia) and Matra (CAS.CADE), as well as companies like Dataquest which want to keep abreast of technological trends.

In great demand

Membership of the club, though, by no means necessarily implies that a vendor has immediate plans to put systems supporting OLE for D&M on the market. Conversely, the fact that other software houses are not in the club certainly does not indicate that they are not also working on similar developments.

No false conclusions

However, the wide-ranging debate within DMAC does justify the conclusion that interest in cross-process and cross-application standardization of graphical software is far greater than anyone could have imagined until a short while ago, and certainly greater than the Intergraph developers had anticipated.

Unexpectedly high level of interest

Let us now turn to the actual extensions to the OLE mechanism. Figure 19 earlier in the book showed the internal structure of OLE/COM. We can refer to this diagram again to illustrate where Intergraph's add-ons fit in.

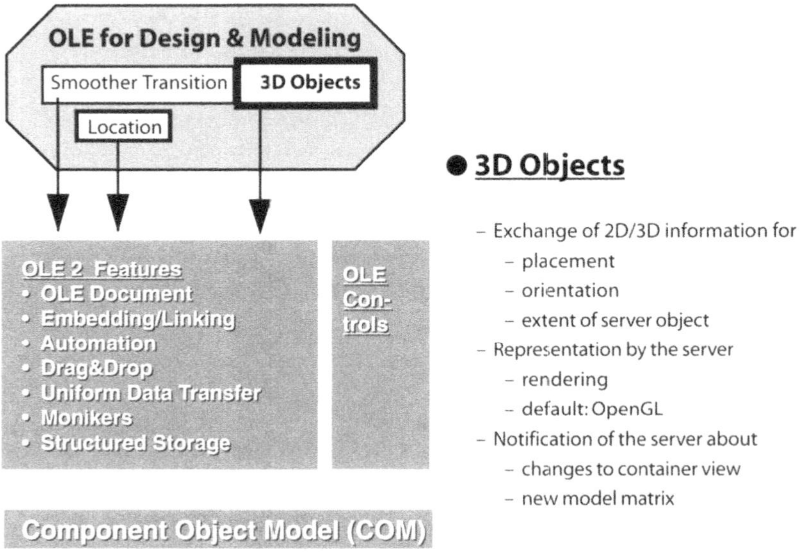

OLE for Design & Modeling

Smoother Transition | **3D Objects**

Location

OLE 2 Features
* OLE Document
* Embedding/Linking
* Automation
* Drag&Drop
* Uniform Data Transfer
* Monikers
* Structured Storage

OLE Controls

Component Object Model (COM)

● **3D Objects**

– Exchange of 2D/3D information for
  – placement
  – orientation
  – extent of server object
– Representation by the server
  – rendering
  – default: OpenGL
– Notification of the server about
  – changes to container view
  – new model matrix

Figure 26: "OLE4DM adds three new interface classes to the compound document model."

Adding 2D and 3D objects to the compound document

OLE for D&M is basically an extension of the compound document mechanism. It allows you to create and edit compound documents containing 2D and 3D objects and to manage the objects regardless of how they were created and what application they come from. The extensions are implemented as three classes of interfaces which function as detailed in the following sections:

1. Describing three-dimensional objects
2. Controlling transitions between objects (both 2D and 3D)
3. Locating pseudo-objects

3.1 Objects in Space

3D objects

These days, more and more applications are being designed to model three-dimensional physical objects. Consequently, it is growing ever more important to ensure that real 3D information can be exchanged between objects and between the associated applications. We are not just talking about communications within the CAD world, either: beyond that we have to consider the whole field of product development, and beyond that again, communications on an enterprise-wide basis. So the issue of OLE extensions is by no means of interest only to CAD developers and users.

3D graphics take off

The new interfaces let objects and containers take full advantage of the third dimension. This includes exchanging 2D and 3D information: if the OLE for D&M specifications are followed, a 3D container can insert 2D objects, and a 3D representation can be inserted in a 2D document.

2D to 3D
and vice versa

The first extension is a definition of *3D (three-dimensional) objects*. It allows a container which understands 3D information to determine the spatial extent of a 3D object and hence its relation to other elements in the container. It also allows a 2D container capable of processing three dimensions to establish the correct view of the object.

Defining the object

The procedure is simple and is in keeping with the general principle of the OLE world. A client wishing to insert an object first addresses that object as an *IOleObject* and then asks via the *QueryInterface* whether it has an interface named *IOle3DObject*. If it does not, it is treated as a 2D object. The *IOle3DObject* interface is implemented in the object and it is addressed by the container. This interface points to a set of functions or methods which can be used at the time when the object is initialized or loaded.

Are you a 3D object?

First the dimensions of the object are checked (*GetExtent*). Every 3D object must always also provide 2D extents, to allow it to be used in a 2D document. Irrespective of which system of coordinates and units of measurement the

How high, how wide,
how long?

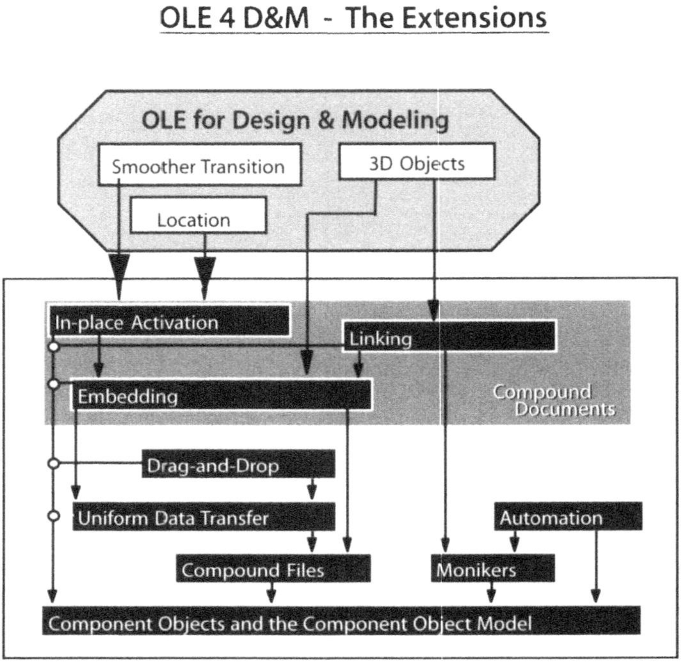

OLE 4 D&M - The Extensions

Figure 27: "The position of the first class of interfaces as part of the OLE extensions."

server uses to manage the object, the OLE extension specifies that all objects must communicate their extent to the outside world in meters. The container then transforms the returned dimensions into its own system of coordinates and where necessary also into its own units if they differ from the standard unit (meters).

The usual   A *default view* (*GetDefaultView*) is the view of a 3D object that a 2D container uses by default. However, it is the server application which specifies which will be the default view, and this may be any possible view of the 3D object.

At the user's discretion   The *SetView* function allows a 3D object to be displayed in a 2D container in other views than the default view. If this function is supported by the object, it is a simple matter to switch from an isometric view to a top

Figure 28: see Color Sction

view or side view, or even to define multiple links to the same object, each with a different view.

A further interface is needed to define the graphical display style. This interface is called *IViewGLObject*. It enables a 3D container to make OpenGL capabilities available to any 3D object. OpenGL has succeeded IrisGL as the industry-standard interface for 2D and 3D graphics accelerators. Further development work is now being monitored by the Architecture Review Board (ARB). This independent grouping, which meets on a quarterly basis, includes representatives from Microsoft, Intel, SGI, Intergraph, DEC, HP, IBM, and Evans & Sutherland.

Standard graphics

Here again we encounter the communication mechanism that we have often met before. The user of the object calls the standard OLE interface *IViewObject* and then asks via QueryInterface whether *IViewGLObject* is supported as well. If it is, the container can request the object to render itself in accordance with the OpenGL conventions. If the interface is not supported, the container must be able to display the object in two dimensions within the 3D space.

Do you know OpenGL?

However, this specification does not restrict applications to OpenGL-style rendering. Every software vendor or developer can support and use other rendering mechanisms; and if others use these as well, they may also form the basis for graphical representation among disparate applications.

As you like it

3.2 Objects in Transit

Transitions between (2D and 3D) objects

Now let's turn to the way a 3D CAD session actually works and consider the fundamental problems that a designer prepared to take full advantage of the technology can solve using special-purpose OLE extensions.

In practice

As a user of a 3D modeling system, you are normally working on a number of different physical objects, and

More than one object

under OLE these objects will all be in one container. You have to be able to access all of the objects, not just one of them; but only the one you are currently editing needs to be active.

Smooth transition

As the number of applications used in combination grows, and as more increasingly complex objects with increasingly complicated interrelationships need to be managed in a single container, it is all the more important to the end user that changing from one object to another, switching between active and inactive object representation, should proceed as quickly and inconspicuously as possible.

Bigger equals slower

In practice a physical model, in mechanical design for example, typically breaks down into various individual parts with fixed relationships to each other. The larger the assemblies, the longer you have to wait for the image to be built up, obscured edges to be computed, etc., if the entire model is active at all times.

More transparency

Furthermore, 3D modeling in particular demands the existence of object boundaries other than the rectangular types hitherto available under OLE and expects objects to be superimposed, without necessarily obscuring each other – after all, they may also be transparent. These requirements likewise cannot be satisfied by OLE as implemented for office applications.

Complete picture

One other difference: when an object is being edited in a 3D modeling application, the usual, sensible procedure is for the entire working surface of the screen to be available for displaying the model, not just one part of it in a separate window, adequate as that may be in other applications. There are diverse interdependencies between the various elements of a model, and editing one object often has a direct impact on other areas.

The container is in charge

Consequently, activating the 3D object should not cause the overall view to change. That would lead to confusion. Thus the requirement with regard to in-place activation of 3D objects is that the special menus of the server application should still appear, but that control of the actual screen workspace, the presentation of the whole model to the user, must remain the responsibility of the container.

Multiple-views

A further limitation of the original OLE interfaces becomes evident if you consider applications which allow

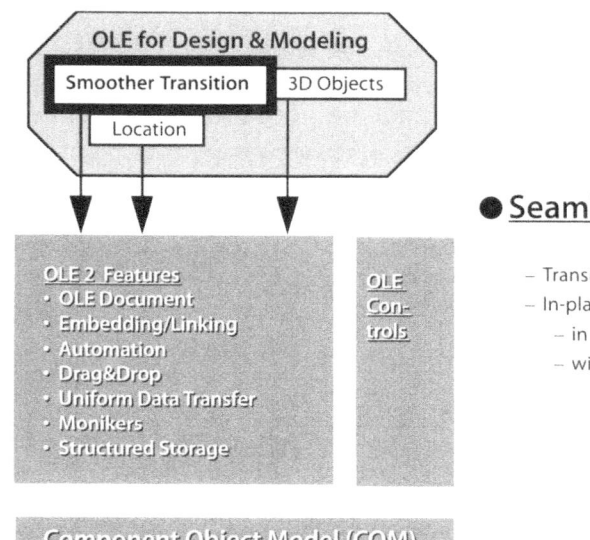

Figure 29: "The second OLE4DM interface class. It allows useful work to be done with CAD objects in a container."

you not only to display several views at once but to have them all active at the same time, too. The user is then of course able to select an enlarged detail in one view and switch with the pointer to another detail window in order to continue the selection process and identify a further discrete geometrical point.

New interfaces had to be specified to meet all these requirements. They were implemented in the following way:

When initialized, the object asks the container for the views in which it supports in-place activation. The object then creates instances known as *child views* corresponding to each of these views. Each new view has exactly the same extents as the corresponding container view. These *pseudo-views* allow the object to react to movements of the mouse pointer, but otherwise they are totally unobtrusive, i.e. invisible. At this stage the server controls all the events that the user triggers from a menu or with the mouse, or the *user interface* generally, and it also controls the appearance of the object being edited.

Views and their children

No chance of misunderstanding

This ensures that the server always receives the event (e.g. a mouse click) and that clicking outside the active object does not deactivate it, as is normally the case with OLE 2. In fact, it is now the server functionality that determines the response to an event, which might be to select some other element in the container, for example.

Not like "normal" OLE

That is a fundamental difference compared to existing OLE applications, where the uniform behavior for activation is triggered by a single mouse click and in-place activation of the server application is initiated by a double click on an object. Double-clicking on a worksheet, for example, invokes the associated spreadsheet program and displays the "Worksheet" object in the active frame. In this case deactivation is simply a matter of clicking outside the rectangular object frame.

Interpretation allowed

This behavior cannot be maintained when working with 3D objects. After all, in a 3D container, i.e. in space, what do we mean when we say "outside the object"? Even if an active object is indicated by a cuboidal outline incorporating the outermost dimensions, the user can never be sure exactly what the mouse pointer is pointing at. It could be the active object or its "frame", but it might equally well be a point located far below it or above it in space.

New approach to the problem

In traditional 3D modeling the solution to this problem was to keep the whole model active at all times. A mouse click then typically inverted the color of the element affected, and if more than one element was affected, you could keep clicking until you found the one you wanted.

If we do not want to keep the whole model active, and if above all we are no longer ready to accept the associated performance penalties, we have to look for a different solution.

Temporary fix?

In the OLE for D&M specifications defined to date, a temporary solution has been chosen. To deactivate an object in a 3D container you press the <Esc> key. In addition, the server application can provide suitable menu items for ending the editing process.

Seeking council

The developers at Intergraph, however, consider it highly probable that consultations within the DMAC framework will come up with a general rule for a standardized approach more like that adopted in 2D documents under OLE to replace the <Esc> command, which is also used for other purposes,

In general terms, extending OLE in this respect involves the same procedure as was described in rather more detail in section 3.1. The appropriate 3D interface is activated by way of the standard OLE interfaces and the ubiquitous QueryInterface. The specifications tell the developer exactly what steps have to be taken, and in what order, to ensure that the overall behavior is as a user would expect under OLE.

Rules of association

3.3 Pseudo-Operations

Locating pseudo-objects

The third class of interfaces in the OLE extensions relates to the information that one object makes available to other objects or to the container.

When combining various objects which come from several applications and may also feature complicated interdependencies, you need to have more information about the objects than simply their external dimensions and the server which is responsible for them. A simplified form of imaging is not good enough, and simply "dragging" an object from the server into the container is inadequate.

More details required

Objects must be able to find space that they can share in the container. Users must be capable of locating them and relating them to each other, and they must have access to information encapsulated in the objects.

Access control

For example: To activate and edit a water tank on a layout plan, you need more than just its visual appearance. You need to be able to identify physical components such as pumps and discharge pipe connectors. However, this information is part of the encapsulated data which initially is available only to the server application. Thus specifications

Tank attachments

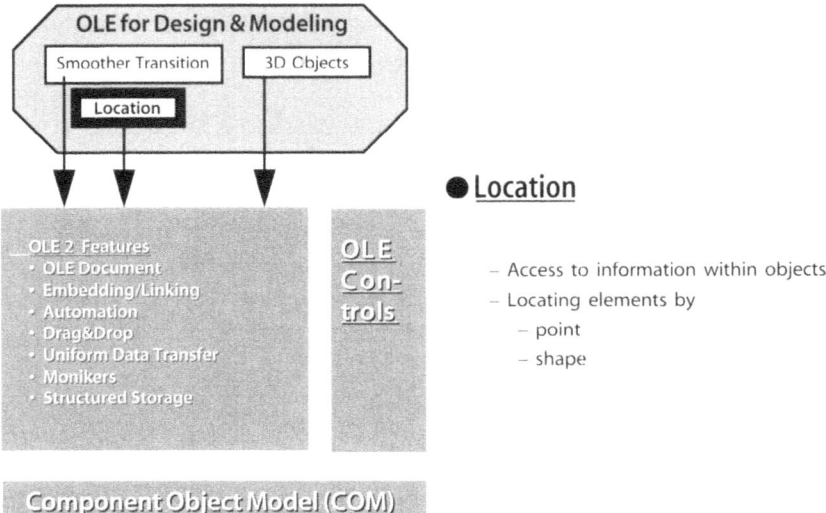

Figure 30: "The third interface class of OLE for Design & Modeling. Without the ability to access the elements of objects and the information they contain, the OLE principle is not a viable proposition in the CAE environment. "

are required to define how, in what form and to what extent such information is to be made accessible to the container or to any other object.

Where one object needs to know something about another

Here, too, the original OLE concept is inadequate. In word processing there is no need to reference individual components of a graphic directly. To modify an object in a conventional 2D container you initially simply have to activate it. This does not involve exchanging information between objects, other than that relating to position and size. That is not the case in 3D modeling and in graphical applications in general.

To illustrate, let us take another example from the field of mechanical design. You need to load an object that has been created in a customer's foreign application. It might be the fender of an automobile, into which you now have to fit the headlight.

Making the connections

Even if this does not necessarily involve modifying the geometry supplied by the customer's server, you will always need to know the geometrical reference points and the surfaces where the part you are supplying comes

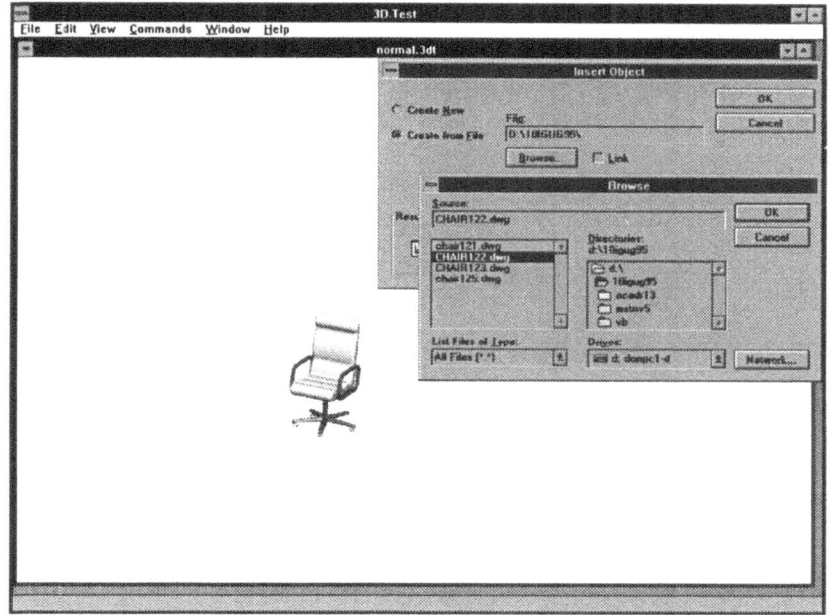

Figure 31: "The 3D model of a chair, created with AutoCAD, is loaded in AutoCAD DWG format, unconverted, by an OLE4DM-based application."

into contact with the bodywork. Thus when fashioning your 3D model, perhaps with a different application, you need to be able to refer directly to the geometrical elements or components of the object that you have received and inserted in your container.

You have to be able to select a geometrical component of the foreign object and use it as a point of reference for a modeling action of your own.

Select and connect

This use of relative references between different objects is in truth only the minimum requirement for CAD to be deployed professionally in an OLE environment. There are far more extensive requirements: how are intersections and other operations involving disparate objects to be implemented successfully without the exchange of the significant information, both geometrical and nongeometrical?

Minimum requirement

Figure 32: see Color Section

What do you have to offer?

The interface specifications for OLE for D&M define the necessary conventions for the first fundamental stage in locating specific elements of an object. A mouse click causes the container application to ask an object for information about certain geometric elements. The reply takes the form of a list of pointers to all the elements that the server application can provide which match the criteria. In the case which requires the least effort from the server but is also the least helpful to the user, this might simply be a list of all the object's elements.

The interface responsible for this aspect is called *IOleLocate*, and it adds a new class to the original set of OLE interfaces.

Point and shape

On this basis, there are currently two mechanisms for locating elements. One goes by the name of *PointLocate*, and it returns all those elements of the identified object which intersect with a defined point or boreline. The other is named *ShapeLocate*, and it references all geometric elements which intersect with a defined plane or shape.

Good foundations

So now the most important conditions are in place for different vendors in the field of graphical applications to develop systems and system components capable of communicating with each other on the basis of OLE for D&M.

Unresolved issues

The issues for which there is as yet no unified solution but only a temporary fix are the questions of visual representation/rendering (OpenGL and/or others ?) and of deactivation (instead of <Esc>). The developers at Intergraph have intentionally left these points open so as not to leave anyone on the sidelines by over-hastily formalizing specific details.

Initial standard: ACIS SAT

Initially, the same applied to the definition of a standard data exchange format. Now, though, consensus has been reached within DMAC on an initial standard. The members of DMAC have agreed to adopt SAT, the format of the ACIS geometry kernel, currently used to exchange data between some 50 ACIS-based applications. It seems probable that STEP and some other commonly used formats will be added later.

Publication of SAT

The background to this agreement was the decision of ACIS vendor Spatial Technology to make SAT open to all, thereby allowing objects in this data structure to be read and written without the need for a converter. In 1995 the ACIS SAT specifications were published in printed form. They can be obtained electronically from the following address:

ftp.spatial.com
and
http://www.spatial.com/spatial

There will also be a SAT Clipboard format, provided by DMAC. This will enable 2D and 3D objects from different systems to be moved and copied from one document to another using the Clipboard, i.e. the Cut and Paste mechanism.

Clipboard SAT

4 Enhancements

4 Enhancements

In the previous chapter we looked at the actual extensions that are accessible throughout the world under the name of OLE for Design and Modeling to anyone interested in developing OLE-compatible CAD or GIS software. They form the basis for extending to the world of graphical applications all the benefits of drag and drop, cut and paste, embedding, linking and in-place editing, in other words all the mechanisms supporting interoperability between different application systems.

Now OLE works with CAD, too

However, it will not have escaped attentive readers that these extensions in fact comprise only the indispensable cross-process and cross-application specifications, not the solution to *all* the problems that have arisen.

Essential but not sufficient

In particular, three problems remain unsolved even after the introduction of OLE for D&M. First there is still the problem of object relationships, for example the constraints (which can sometimes be parameterized) that govern the relationships between geometrical elements. This topic is covered below in the section on the relationships model in the Jupiter environment.

Constraints under OLE4DM

Second there is the question of how to approach data management and data security with regard to complex graphical objects and of whether the tools and databases available today are capable of providing the *persistence* required of 3D models.

What kind of security?

Finally, there is the problem of dealing with software systems which do not use the OLE mechanism but were written in the old style in a wide range of different languages. End users may not want to do without these systems when switching to OLE technology, or they may have to continue working with the CAD models created with them. The section on wrappers illustrates the methods which allow for interoperability in the Jupiter environment even in conjunction with systems which are absolutely not OLE-aware.

Coexistence or conflict?

4.1 Relationships

No relation

As we established at the beginning of the book, the object model underlying the OLE/COM mechanism makes no provision for defining fixed relationships between objects beyond the simple relationship of container to object and of object to server application. We likewise concluded that this issue is of primary importance for all applications in the field of CAD/CAM and GIS.

Interesting approach

OLE for D&M has not solved this problem. Like many other issues it is in fact an application-specific issue that each development team has to address for its own application. Intergraph has, though, come up with an approach which looks decidedly interesting and promises to offer a far-reaching solution to the problem.

Badly mapped

In conjunction with physical models in particular and graphical objects in general, the main shortcoming of inheritance models is their limited ability to map complex interrelationships. All the cases described in section 1.3 involved some kind of tree structure, or hierarchical dependencies. Relationships of this type are based on the assumption that it is possible to determine in absolute terms which value is the stage of origin and which is the result. There must be a fixed *parent-child* relationship.

False assumption

Unfortunately, this assumption is fundamentally inapplicable to graphical applications, both on practical grounds and for a reason which is in the very nature of graphical objects.

Unknown quantities

The details come later

The practical grounds relate to an issue that has long been avoided by application builders and users alike. This is the fact that during product development most of the geometrical and non-geometrical properties of a model are subject to constant change and are not truly fixed until the product is released.

However, with conventional CAD systems – 2D ones anyway and to date most 3D ones - you could not really do useful work until the detailing of the model was largely complete, which basically meant at the time when the final drawing was produced. So CAD was purely tangential to the most significant stages of product development where all the important decisions are made – concept, design and drafting. Design work here was and is mostly done with special-purpose systems barely capable of communicating meaningfully with the other CAx applications.

Exclusion zone

Nobody finds that satisfactory, however, and the success of products like Pro/ENGINEER proves that modern product development depends on support from 3D modelers at a far earlier point and is in need of systems which allow the engineer considerably greater flexibility in making changes to models than earlier system generations.

More flexibility required

Thus if the next generation of object-based software is to achieve progress on this point, what is required is a method capable of managing variable and unpredictable relationships between all the components of a model.

No going back

There must be no need to specify from the very beginning whether a bore hole depends on this particular surface or that. There must be no need for complete remodeling simply because one element of a model which originally had other elements attached to it is deleted.

Freedom demanded by the designer

Not so trivial

The second reason for the failure of conventional rules of inheritance in the CAD context can be illustrated by a few simple examples:

1. You define a line in the form of a vector by setting a point of origin and an angle to the horizontal. You then create a second line parallel to the first and at a fixed distance from it. You justifiably expect that in subsequent manipulations it will be irrelevant which of the two lines you select and move or rotate – the other,

Equivalence relation

whichever it is, must track its movements and maintain the condition *parallel.* Yet which line is in this case the parent and which is the child? The dependency works both ways and cannot be logically resolved in one direction.

Dependency relation

2. Figure 34 shows another example of simple dependencies: A line intersects a curve. The outcome is the point of intersection common to the two original elements. Its position must change to reflect each change to the position of the line or the curve.

3. In Figure 35, this point of intersection is declared as the center of a circle with a defined radius, touched by a tangent (L2) running parallel to the existing line (L1). We observe that if the new line (the tangent) is moved, the coordinates of the point of intersection change as well. Yet there is no direct relationship between the point of intersection and the parallel line. Moreover, even this example, simple as it is, shows that there are no more one-way dependencies. A change you make to one element may result in modifications which ultimately again affect the element you changed first.

Reality is much more complicated

Complicated as this case already looks, it is in truth only a foretaste of the problems facing us in 3D modeling, for example. All we have done is to bring geometrical primitives into relationship with each other as instances of objects. Nevertheless, this example does serve to give some small idea of the complexity of the geometrical problems involved with 3D objects.

Chain reaction

In the real world of 3D applications, things are far more complicated. There, manipulating a single element may result in a whole chain of changes to other elements which ultimately affect the original element again, and it is by no means easy to keep track of all the consequences.

Equivalence Relation

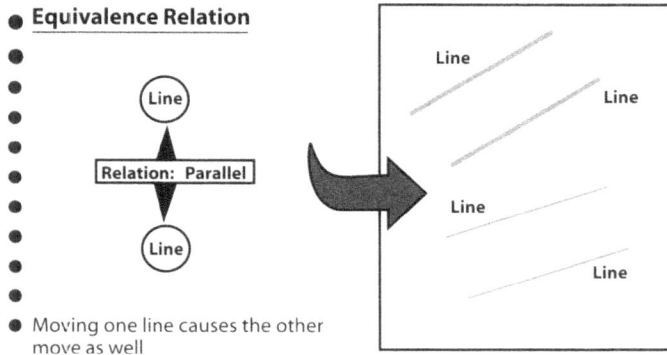

- Moving one line causes the other move as well

Figure 33

Dependency Relation

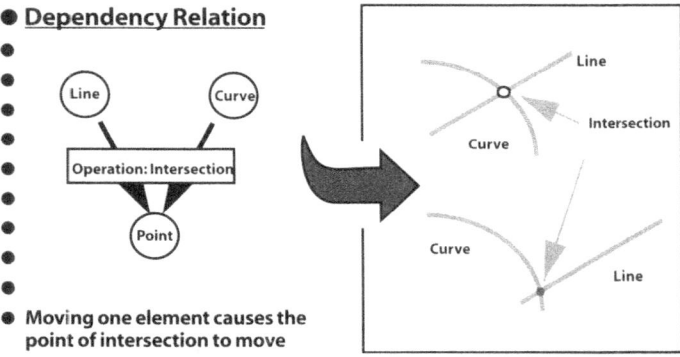

- **Moving one element causes the point of intersection to move**

Figure 34

Associativity Graph

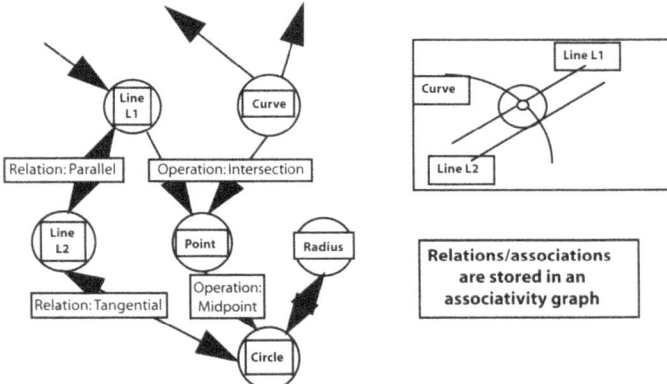

Relations/associations are stored in an associativity graph

Figure 35

Graphs

Associativity graph

The directional tree structure of dependencies is by no means the most generalized form of relationship. The general form of presentation is the graph. At first glance it looks very similar to a finite element analysis mesh. In the context of our CAD model, the nodes would correspond to the individual objects – in the example (Figure 35) to the elements of the 2D representation; the lines between the nodes would represent the relationships or constraints between them; and the network as a whole would correspond to the drawing or to the model of the assembly of the finished product.

Sequential or not

Now we pick out a single element and edit it in place. At this point there are basically two possibilities. Either there is a truly directional dependency between the objects which can be resolved sequentially, or in one or more areas of the graph there are loops which cannot be resolved sequentially. The constraints and dependencies in fact have to be satisfied simultaneously, and ambiguities may even arise if there are a number of correct solutions to the problem.

This method of representation is truly capable of mapping all the theoretically conceivable relationships between any objects. And this is the very method that the Intergraph specialists have chosen as the basis for their relationships model.

Reasonable solution

The question that remains to be answered is this: what happens if the second case occurs and there are a number of correct solutions to choose from? Well, it is something like what happens in real life when you have a choice between alternatives. You delimit the problem and narrow it down to the solution which seems the most reasonable in the light of all available evidence. In our case that means splitting up the cycle and forcing it to be directional.

Relationship management

This problem has to be solved in very specific terms, so it cannot be left up to a generalist. Instead, you need to turn to whichever advisers are best qualified to deal with each type of problem situation that arises. In this context Intergraph refers to *solvers*, which are created and used within or as extensions to an application on an application-specific or even problem-specific basis.

Solvers

Thus a 2D solver will solve the associativity problems of 2D profiles, and another solver will take care of correct inter-relationships in complex 3D models. Incidentally, software from DCUBED in England has been selected for these two. The overall model of the *Relationship Management System* is designed such that the solvers can come both from outside developers and from in-house sources.

Free choice of the best solution

Thus the issues of object relationship are resolved in a manner which imposes no restrictions on users with regard to either the size or the complexity of the objects they utilize.

Boundless

The module responsible for *relationship management* in Jupiter applications goes by the name of *ASSOC*, short for associativity. Everything that had to be done to achieve full associativity on earlier systems, using tiresome add-in programs and complicated attribute management routines and always at the cost of considerable performance penalties, all this is handled automatically by *ASSOC*.

Associative

Basically, you can consider the relationship model as an object model together with the actual objects, the difference being that in this instance relationships are the only things that play any part.

Relationship model

Intergraph will be offering ASSOC as part of the development platforms for various industry-specific applications. That means that developers working on these platforms will find that one of the central problems of modern object technology has been solved for them in advance, leaving them to concentrate on their primary objectives.

4.2 Persistence

Known identity

As promised, we now return to the question of data security. After all, what is the use of even the best object relationship management mechanism if there is no guarantee that every object can always preserve its identity and ensure its own survival? Or to put it another way, a model like ASSOC will be totally ineffective unless every object is uniquely identifiable at all times.

The file as object space

In conventional CAD applications, all the data of a model was stored in *files*. More recent object-oriented systems have continued to use this approach as well, managing the object along with its interfaces, methods and data in "object spaces" which are files in all but name.

Anticipating Cairo

The Jupiter project is approaching it in a different way. In keeping with the policy of basing as much as possible directly on OLE/COM, the structured storage technique has been selected as the basis for regulating data storage for technical objects, extending OLE for D&M and anticipating *Cairo*.

Compound models

The approach to storing 3D models within applications based on the Jupiter concept is the same as in the general model for compound documents described in section 2.3.5.

Clusters for speed

Related parts, elements or assemblies are grouped to form *clusters* within the compound file. That enhances performance when searching for specific data and minimizes the time required to access the models.

Identity preserved

Direct application of the moniker concept now also allows suitably designed CAD applications to store the models that you create securely on a unique and permanent basis, or for as long as seems useful and appropriate from the product development viewpoint.

As specified by the underlying OLE/COM mechanism, data security is guaranteed globally for all objects which observe this convention.

4.3 Wrappers

Here we touch on a rather tricky aspect of the whole technology, affecting not just modeling applications but the OLE world in general. OLE/COM is a mechanism, or rather a specification, which draws strength from the fact that it is made the basis of applications on the broadest possible scale. Not every application that "supports OLE" ranks equally in this respect. An application can implement part of the mechanism for its own purposes and leave out or redefine other parts. To that extent the user within an OLE environment is considerably dependent on application builders showing serious interest in making the most of the opportunities for interoperability that are now available.

What does OLE-capable mean?

However, OLE does also provide a basic facility for communicating with differently designed, proprietary or partially closed systems, and this is the technique that will be used to enable traditional graphical applications to co-exist with OLE-based programs. It involves cocooning conventional non-OLE software in a layer of OLE features to make it amenable to OLE operations, and this OLE layer is known as a *wrapper*.

Allowing for cooperation

As an extra enhancement to OLE for Design and Modeling Applications, Intergraph has created the *OLE data server* principle to provide wrapper functionality.

Imagine you are an plant designer working with an OLE-based application and in the process of designing a new plant. You can see the plant as being your container, holding a very large number of objects.

CAD containers

Now you would like to make use of existing resources, taking various objects such as machine parts, motors and pumps and incorporating them as ready-made elements in your new plant . This library of available parts has been created with an "old-style" system, such as PDS, TIGRIS/ DYNAMO, MicroStation or an AutoCAD application.

Old CAD library

The problem is obvious. The objects you want to integrate have a different data format; they are unaware of the OLE/COM interface rules; and their server application is not accustomed to exchanging its models with other

Not used to working together

OLE applications can use existing CAD data as OLE objects without conversion

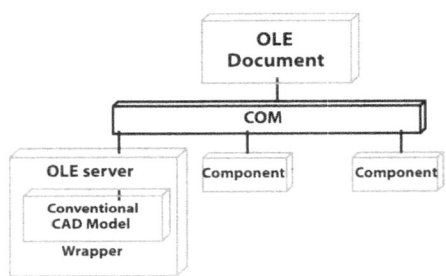

Figure 36: "Wrappers encapsulate conventional CAD data to bring it into line with the rules of the Component Object Model."

applications, except by the roundabout method of conversion to another format.

In practical terms that means that drag and drop, in-place editing and any of the other OLE conveniences will fail because none of the objects being activated has any idea what a *QueryInterface* is.

Wrap it up   This handicap can, however, be overcome quite easily. The object *old system X* itself is simply encapsulated according to all the rules of the OLE art. It is placed in a wrapper which complies in all respects with the OLE and OLE for D&M interface specifications, and from then on the objects of the old system can communicate with the new system as if they had always done so. In other words, the OLE/COM paradigm does not require the rewriting of existing program code, but instead allows specific functionality of conventional CAD systems to be made executable retroactively under the conditions of modern object technology.

EMS objects   That includes in-place activation capability. You can,
under OLE   for example, insert an EMS model into an OLE for D&M application, and if you then double-click on it, the *OLE data server* will supply the commands you need to view, position and use the model without otherwise modifying your screen. It is not until you press <Esc> that the special menu items disappear and are replaced by those of the container. Similarly, a Catia data server can be implemented, allowing 3D surface and solid model objects to

be imported in native format and, following in-place activation, combined with other objects and manipulated on screen in a variety of ways.

In short, *OLE data servers* can be written for all conventional CAD systems; and in principle anyone can write them, even the customer. There is just one condition: the data structure of the system or component that you want to wrap must have been published. That, though, is the case with most CAD systems today anyway.

Anyone can do it!

It does, however, make far more sense for application builders to write OLE data servers for their own (old) applications. That is because the exact form of an OLE data server governs the extent to which the OLE mechanism is supported and to which the user has access to specific functions in the new environment.

What is fascinating about *wrappers* or *OLE data servers* is doubtless the fact that for the first time in the history of graphical software development it creates the conditions for modern technology to coexist with legacy systems. And that lets individual users protect past investments and also puts them in a position to define for themselves the point at which they switch fully to the new technology.

You've never seen anything like it!

Merging Models

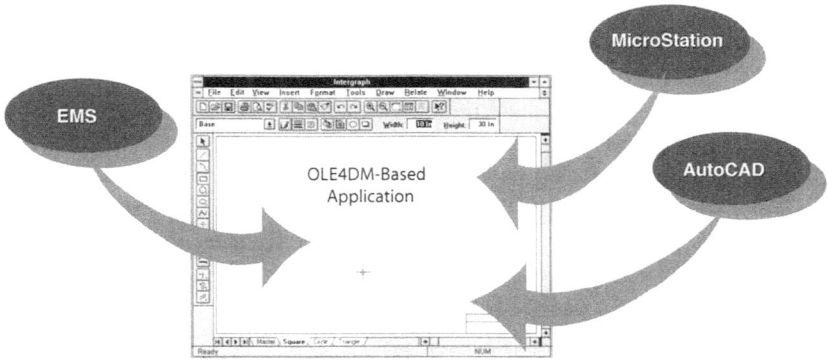

Figure 37: "The principle is clear: objects from different systems and with different data structures can be used in the same container – using drag and drop, in-place activation and all the other benefits of OLE."

Two programs at once   If there are old and new applications on the same computer (or on the network, once the restrictions currently relating to OLE and networking have been eliminated), using OLE technology it is even possible to double-click on an "old" object and activate the associated wrapped application itself without quitting the program currently running.

Anything goes   The OLE/COM paradigm actually offers more possibilities than will probably ever be implemented. It would in theory be quite possible to create "full" servers to make the full functionality of conventionally written software available, which in turn would allow, say, embedded objects to be edited and geometrically modified without having to be converted first. In the coming years it will become apparent whether and to what extent such an approach makes sense and is demanded by the market.

The first batch   To start with, anyway, Intergraph will be supplying OLE data servers for EMS, MicroStation, AutoCAD, Technovision, Proren and generally for SAT, STEP and IGES objects. User requirements will be the primary factor in determining which others will be developed.

5

Toolkits

5 Toolkits

The chief principles are defined, the interfaces are specified, and the main problems are solved. However, three requirements are still missing. Firstly is the actual application environment and of course the 2D and 3D objects that can be used for modeling, designing and developing. Secondly are the applications themselves and the formulation of rules governing the behavior of objects in response to commands, menus and mouse events. Thirdly is a user-friendly development environment which saves software development organizations of all sizes from having to reinvent the wheel when creating their own OLE components.

Developer's toolkit

5.1 Framework

The executive suite

As part of the Jupiter project, Intergraph provides a management module known as the *Application Executive*. This relieves the application designer of all tasks which are not directly to do with the application. The Application Executive defines the display, manages the paths, and takes care of object relationships and data security. At the same time it guarantees optimum access to all the required Windows modules: Mail, File Open or Print, to name but a few examples. Lastly the Application Executive controls the redefinition of objects, commands, functions, menus and dialog boxes.

What every application needs

Application Executive

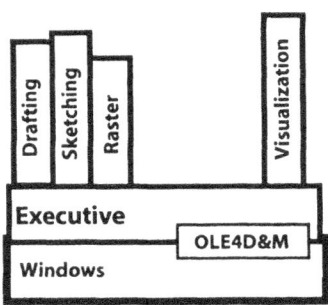

Figure 38: "This diagram shows how the Application Executive fits into the Windows and OLE for Design & Modeling environment and what functions it supports."

What Intergraph is
developing for itself
and others

Intergraph's motives for introducing this powerful platform as a basis for all future software systems were on the one hand primarily for its own benefit. On the other hand, though, this framework of development tools can be provided to developers, development groups and end users that are interested, assuming the appropriate business cases, support capabilities and organizational structures are available.

A mere 0.4 MB!

Incidentally, an impressive indication of how far the development methodology has been optimized is provided by the size of the Application Executive. The entire set of tools actually weighs in at no more than about 400 KB. So what exactly does it contain?

Yet another set of
interfaces

It comprises three interfaces that are of significance to programmers of new applications: *DCX, DNX* and *DEX.* The first two help to define the range of services that the application offers to users, while the third is used to describe new object types.

Dynamics in action

The abbreviation *DCX* stands for *Dynamic Command Extensions*. Here the developer writes the primary functional code. *DCX* is used to define the actual features or functionality of an application, the commands that give the user access to these functions, and the results that they produce.

What the user can do

DNX stands for *Dynamic Environment Extensions*. These affect only the user interface, specifying which menus are offered, how the commands can most conveniently be made available to the user, which icon bars and toolboxes are to appear when and where, and what options the user has for customizing the interface to suit particular applications or special requirements.

How the user can do it

Dynamic results

To solve certain problems of relationships among objects it may be necessary to call upon a specific *solver*. It is however also possible for an action to lead directly to the third of the named interfaces.

With or without sidestep

The single interface which then implements the results of the activities involved is named *DEX*, which stands for *Dynamic Entity Extensions*.

Dynamic elements

DEX allows the application developer to control which entities or objects can be created as the result of specific function calls. The developer can define whether and how they can be deleted, modified and copied; whether and how they can be extended; how they are to be represented; and what relationships they have with other objects.

Delete, modify and copy

Using the Application Executive, all that programmers really need to do to ensure that their applications will integrate smoothly with the OLE/COM world is to make sure that these interfaces are accessed and implemented correctly. Furthermore, this framework is independent of the type of application involved. It can be used in the

Relatively simple

creation of GIS components, but it also supports the programming of architecture applications or mechanical design systems.

In short, this framework is the true nucleus of any application designed in full compliance with the rules of the Jupiter concept.

Getting specific

Intergraph has not stopped there, though, but has gone quite some way further in building development environments. So at this point we shall leave questions of general applicability and examine some specific areas of application.

5.2 Services

Services for the developer

Options for the development kernel initially include two sets of modules for solving geometrical problems for applications in different sectors of the market. The basic difference between the sets is that one is intended primarily for two-dimensional graphics applications, the other for 3D object modeling.

All the individual services are optional, above all in the sense that developers can at any time replace them with other services better suited to their own purposes.

2D services

Use what is already there

These comprise three components designed to make solutions easier to find in three major areas: *Render* (for optimum representation), *Symbology* (a symbol library) and *Constraints* (for managing parametric relationships).

For these services – by now it almost goes without saying – nothing has been built from scratch if it has already been developed in a suitable form elsewhere.

ACIS family

Thus the *Constraints* service, for example, is derived from the *Dimensional Constraint Manager (DCM)* designed by DCUBED in Cambridge, which is being developed in close cooperation with the ACIS Solid Modeling Geometry Kernel and like ACIS is used as a standard module in numerous application programs.

3D services

The *Constraints* service is also to be found amongst the *3D services*, as the basis for relationship management among 3D solids; and logically enough, the 3D modeling kernel that we find here is ACIS itself. ACIS, now used in well over 100 applications, has achieved the status of a *de facto* standard. Coming from the same origin as ROMULUS, ACIS does not just represent the accumulated wisdom of 25 years of 3D CAD development. It is also one of the fastest and most robust kernels currently available.

The kernel: ACIS

Since deciding to implement this kernel, Intergraph has given much thought to identifying points at which cross-

Effective cooperation

The Jupiter Development Platform

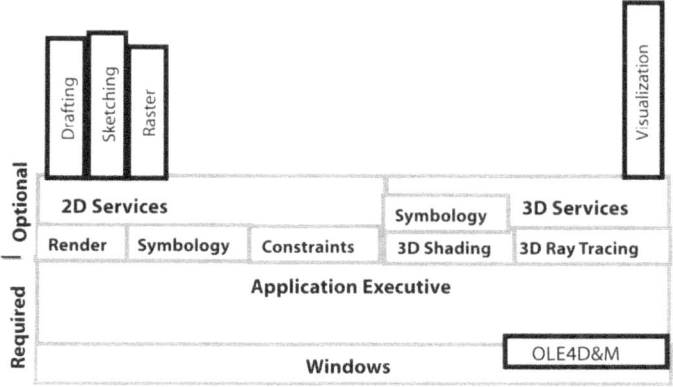

Figure 39: "The 2D and 3D services are available as generally applicable tools to all developers looking to build applications based on the Jupiter concept."

fertilization could save effort and increase the benefits for both parties.

Surfaces from Intergraph

Thus the library of surface algorithms put together as part of I/EMS has been offered to Spatial Technology as an extension to the ACIS model builder. It now replaces the surface component previously used with ACIS and provides many enhancements for developers and users of ACIS-based systems.

Enhancements

The Huntsville team has also enhanced the ACIS kernel used within the Jupiter project by adding a series of features which are not part of the standard functionality of the solid modeler. We shall be returning to this point later when we look at a number of examples from the field of mechanical design.

The tools supplied for 3D applications also include rendering and symbology components.

5.3 Add-Ons

One, two, many tools

Finally, leaving questions of geometry aside, there is a whole range of useful components which are needed with varying regularity, depending on the application involved. For this purpose Intergraph creates a series of tools as optional extras, geared to the requirements of the given application.

Here, there and everywhere

Of course this library is only a start, and it is likely to expand greatly over the coming years as new components of general applicability are created in the course of development work on new applications. That means that it will also incorporate components developed by vendors other than Intergraph.

On the shelves

For the present, the contents of the library are: *DocMgr*, a *Cairo*-compliant document manager for CAD systems; a *Plot* module for outputting graphics and 3D models; Translate, ODBC, Query and many more components. In addition, information such as industry-specific expertise and specialized technological knowledge is available in the

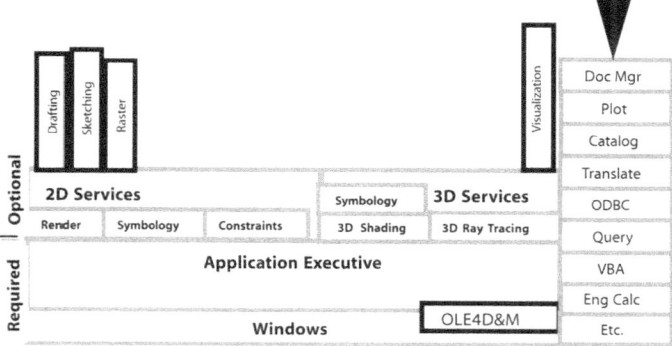

The Jupiter Development Platform
with Supplementary Components
Not Classifiable as 2D or 3D

Figure 40

form of ready-made modules suitable for incorporation in a total system solution.

So all in all the coming years will see Intergraph offering a series of application-specific development platforms, each comprising the Application Executive, the framework consisting of the Batch Manager and the DCX, DNX and DEX interfaces, plus the 2D and/or 3D services, and optionally other tools as well.

Platforms for different applications

These toolkits are the new style of CAD development platform, built on the back of the OLE/COM mechanism. This style is fundamentally different from anything comparable, whether it be MicroStation or AutoCAD or standards such as ACIS or STEP.

New style of platform

The new environment features no special-purpose, proprietary programming language. All its components have been written using standard tools, either Visual Basic or Visual C++, and can be extended or adapted by anyone using the same standards.

Windows native

There are no proprietary rules forming the actual functional basis for new applications. All new rules are based directly on the Microsoft standards available in millions of copies throughout the world, and they form an integral part of the overall OLE/COM concept.

Optimization Program

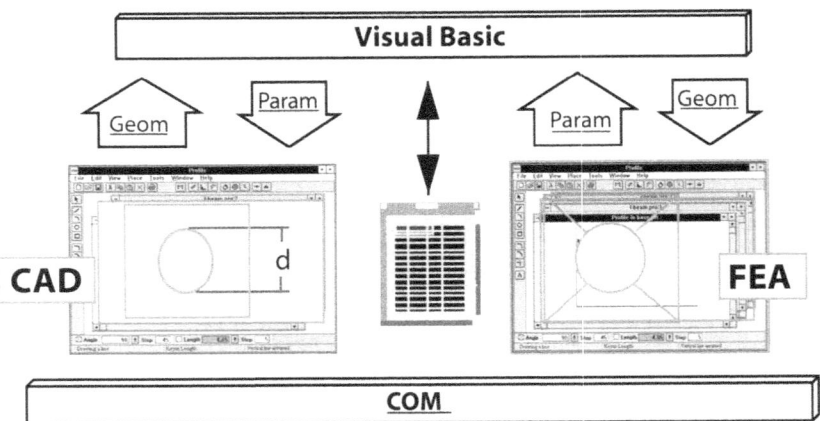

Figure 41: "*Visual Basic as a means of helping users and developers establish direct connections between applications or adapt programs to meet specific needs. In this example, the geometry generated by the CAD system is used for calculations, and the finite element analysis produces parameters which result in an optimization of the geometry.*"

6 Interoperability

6 Interoperability

A t last we have reached the point where all the beauties of object technology can be expressed in terms of practical benefits for users at their screens. Although Intergraph's original point of departure was the same as that of other software houses, i.e. the wish to develop a more powerful, more flexible new generation of applications built up from modular components, this objective can now be pursued with intensified vigor on an unexpectedly firm and broad base.

Open and flexible

Intergraph's commitment to Windows and Windows NT has gained added significance. Apart from the fact that the entire product range is geared to one standardized operating system, there are now other factors serving to unify all future Intergraph products. They will all be based directly on OLE/COM and be written in Visual C++ or Visual Basic, and they will all comply with the rules that have evolved in the course of the Jupiter project and are now also largely accepted as a basis by Microsoft and other vendors.

Windows times two

That not only means that different components are easier to combine, but that all modules will also have a consistent appearance, since they will all be using the same objects at the user interface – from data management through parametric 3D modeling of complex assemblies. And it means that every user of any such product can be sure of making the most of the benefits of Windows, Windows NT and the OLE mechanism.

Useful standardization

And there is one other thing that it means. We can safely assume that all these factors together will greatly speed up product development at Intergraph, as component reusability will now be able to take full effect.

Faster to market?

Those who attended the 1995 meeting of the International IGUG (Intergraph Graphics Users Group) in Huntsville, Alabama, were given some idea of what is in store.

Enthusiastic customers

Practical demonstrations were given of a number of products scheduled to hit the market in the same year. They caused something of a sensation, so great was the difference from the familiar functionality of conventional CAD solutions, Intergraph's own systems included.

A brief glance at two of the products presented there will serve as an example of what OLE for D&M can be expected to offer in the next few years.

6.1 Mechanics

Market research   I had the opportunity of talking to Dan Staples, product manager for mechanical design systems, about the motivations and strategies for his part of the market. He told me of a market analysis, carried out by Intergraph a little over three years before, which had had a major impact on defining the current development focus.

Benchmarking blues   Most remarkable was the finding that, almost without exception and irrespective of company size, users were and

Figure 42: "Dan Staples, Mechanics product manager at Intergraph in Huntsville, Alabama."

still are all going about system selection using fundamentally inappropriate benchmarks and asking the wrong questions. As Dan Staples puts it:

"They typically bring along a drawing, which in real life is only what you get as the result of development. They ask for a part to be modeled on the basis of this drawing, and then they want to see how to make assemblies from separate parts and modify them; but in reality the design of the complete product comes first, and that then gets analyzed and broken down into discrete subassemblies and separate parts. It's a tragedy, really. But because until now systems have not supported the actual development process, users have just not been able to make their methods the basis for selection decisions."

The system must support the process

In fact with traditional development methods it was not possible to map processes of this complexity. First a way had to be found to make the individual, elementary modules of the software so simple that they could be used to form the basis for implementing highly complex structures. And so it is that production is about to begin on a mechanical design product which on central issues turns previous approaches upside down – in the most positive sense as far as users are concerned.

Get back to basics to solve complex problems

Starting with the assembly

This product, Solid Edge, can be described as *assembly-oriented*. It is tailored specifically for assembly modeling. This is what Intergraph calls *design in the context of assembly*. Starting with the conception and modeling of a design model it truly allows you to work down from the whole to the details, while having the whole available at all times.

From outline to detail

In the OLE vocabulary that you are now familiar with, we might explain it in the following terms. The assembly environment becomes a container capable of holding a great many individual objects, parts and subassemblies. To edit an object you use the functions that were used to

Model container

create it, which can be activated in-place at any time. Yet the whole model and its structure of relationships, however complex, always remain accessible. In the case of Solid Edge this goes hand in hand with the ability to display the entire assembly structure graphically in a window next to the model, and to use it interactively for editing and display purposes.

True features

Know your place

Another example that Dan Staples cites is the system's ability to handle *true features:* "If you take a closer look at the definable 3D features in traditional CAD systems, you cannot fail to notice that they are still doing simple Boolean operations, with a bit of intelligence added. But the defining characteristic of a feature is supposed to be that it is aware of its boundary conditions and automatically tries to maintain them; and that is something that most applications simply could not handle."

He gives a few examples to illustrate how this problem is solved with the new OLE-based product:

Cumbersome routine

"As a designer, when you define a through-hole, you generally know where the hole begins, but the end is determined by the component that is to have the hole in it. So till now you had to choose dimensions which would at least ensure that the hole would go all the way through. Then the system did a Boolean subtraction of the hole cylinder from the model. This can be a very time-consuming process and can lead to tiresome reiterations if incorrect values are specified.

One-sided intelligence

The way we have solved this problem is that the software itself now finds out where the hole ends. The designer chooses what we call a *one-sided feature* and simply defines the position, diameter and direction of the hole. The application handles the rest.

Wall to wall

Or take the reverse problem. You place a rib in some hollow space. Normally, you have to describe it in such a

Boolean Operation ... and True Features

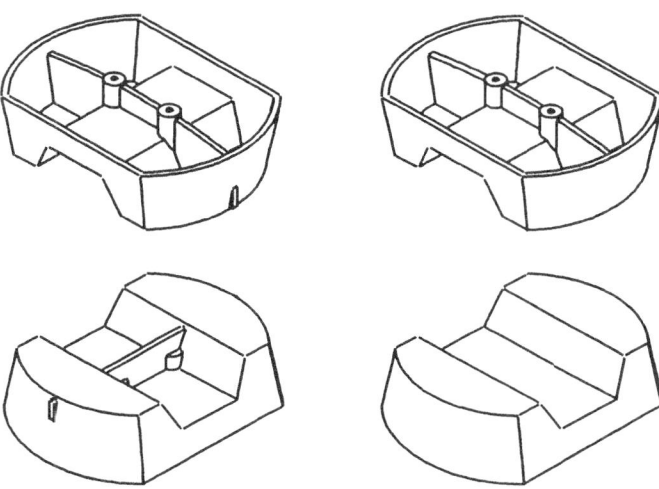

Figure 43: "A typical example of what is meant by 'true features' and how they differ from conventional modeling. In one case, significant manual trimming and cleanup is required, in the other the result is exactly as the designer intended."

way that it is sure to extend beyond the walls at which it is supposed to end, and the actual end of the rib is governed by where it merges with the walls. This, too, is something that an object-oriented application can solve much more elegantly. After all, all the information for the adjoining objects is available. In our system the process is called *filling.* You simply position the rib and describe its shape, and the joins with the model are worked out automatically."

The underlying product philosophy is that 3D objects are fashioned so realistically that many of the routine on-screen activities that used to be required are unnecessary because the system can supply the right information far more quickly and reliably and apply it to the desired operations.

The system knows best

Strategy

In terms of product strategy, Dan Staples identifies three points to which all developments in the field of mechanical design will be geared in the future:

Don't make everything yourself

1. "What to make and what to buy". The chief commandment – and something that can be achieved effectively on the basis of OLE – is that in every development project, with every component and function, you should restrict yourself to making things which do not yet exist elsewhere in a more suitable form.

Industry orientation

2. In line with the market analysis, all products must be tailored very closely to the actual development processes in industry so as to provide optimum support for them.

Standards, standards

3. Finally, high priority must be given to ease of access to all objects, which means basing everything on standards wherever possible. Examples of this approach are the use of ACIS and SAT format, constraints from DCUBED, and using Visual Basic as a tool for designing enhancements.

From general-purpose to special-purpose

Intergraph is adopting a pragmatic approach to the order in which it is gradually providing new products for the various mechanical design application areas. First come the applications for general mechanical engineering, then those for specialized areas such as metalworking and injection molding, and finally modules for tool and mold making and styling functions.

EMS is still with us

Since the traditional programs can coexist with the new applications, the development strategy naturally also embraces the issue of how these old-style CAD products are to be handled. Here, too, the approach is pragmatic. Where appropriate, existing functionality will be imported into the OLE systems from EMS modules, for example. Conversely, future versions of I/EMS will also partly benefit from new developments that offer functional enhancements to the older program.

6.2 Drawing Tools

Imagineer Technical[3] is the name of the first OLE product released by Intergraph. From the outside, it is a very simple, and above all, easily manageable tool for creating simple drawings. However "simple" is not at all the same thing as "primitive" or "weak" in respect of its functionality.

Just as you would imagine

The best way to sum up what it does would be to say that it combines many drawing methods already met in embryonic form in a wide range of other applications and yet manages to do so with an astonishingly small number of commands.

A lot with little effort

The cursor highlights any selectable elements or points in its vicinity that might be of interest to the user. It generally acts like a sensor which always seems to know what the user is intending to do next. Thus small symbols

Intelligent mouse

[3] Intergraph Imagineer Technical is sold under the trademark Intergraph Imagination Engineer in Japan, France, Austria, Belgium, The Netherlands, Luxembourg, Switzerland, Denmark, Finland, Greece, Italy, and Portugal.

- **5 commands**
- **26 mouse clicks**
- **13 key presses**
- **Less than 1 minute**

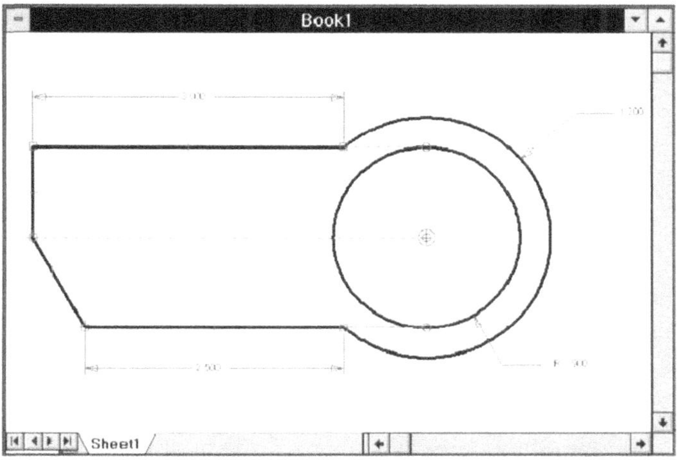

Figure 44: *"An example of the ease of use offered by the new drawing package. If you have a CAD system to hand, you can try counting the commands, mouse clicks and key presses that would be necessary to perform this task."*

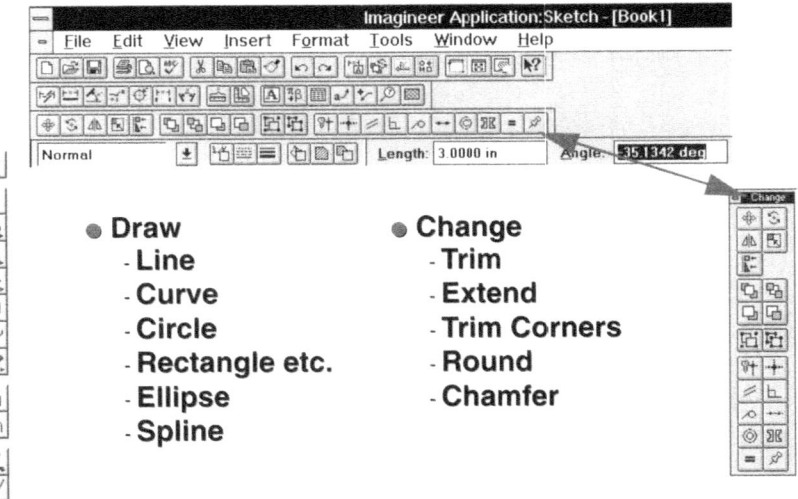

Figure 45: "And that is all there is to the interface of the new system. The intelligence that object technology can provide cuts down on tiresome routine activities and unnecessary input."

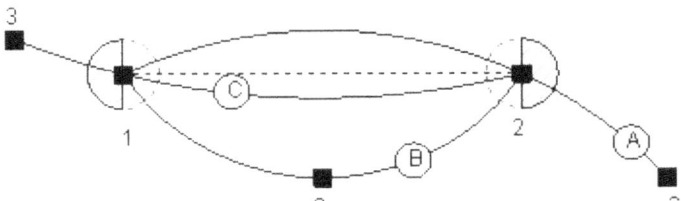

Figure 46: "To draw an arc Imagineer Technical needs just one command. The system itself works out whether the third point set by the user is to be placed between the first two or is intended to be an end point."

appear, without any prompting from the user, to indicate relationships between elements, such as perpendicular or parallel, possible points of contact such as tangents, midpoints or corners, and dimensioning tips for values such as radii and diameters.

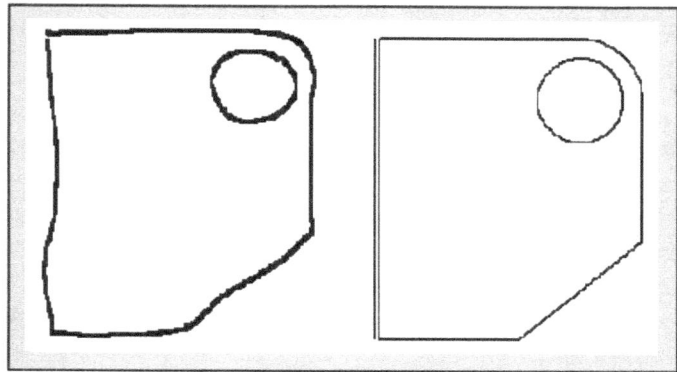

Figure 47: "A tiny example of the intelligence of the new 2D system. The freehand sketch automatically turns into precise geometry. What this diagram cannot show is that the result is there immediately after you issue the command."

Parametric relationships can be defined as required. This is handled by the *Constraints* module, one of the 2D services introduced in section 5.2.   *Parametrics*

A *FreeSketch* function lets you draw rough shapes free-hand and then automatically converts them into precise geometry. That applies not only to straight lines but to arcs, circles and splines as well.   *Exact sketching*

Like one of those ClipArt galleries you find in graphics programs, *Imagineer Technical* offers a library of geometrical objects that you can extend as you wish, even by adding your own components.   *CAD gallery*

To manage the different stages in the production of a drawing the system makes use of drawing sheets. Each time the user makes a modification to a sketch, a new sheet can be inserted which creates a new tab along the bottom of the screen. Then after a series of sessions you can click on these tabs to "page" backwards through your entire design history.   *Sheet by sheet*

One for all

Of course, these are all functions that could also have been implemented without the OLE platform, and the odd one or two are already known to exist in other systems.

Guaranteed exchange

What is new is the ability to combine *Imagineer Technical* freely with other 2D CAD systems. There are already OLE data servers for EMS, MicroStation and AutoCAD, so it is already possible to exchange objects with these three products without any difficulty.

Multipurpose

Thus you can use the package to quickly and conveniently create parametric boundaries, and then pass them on to another program for further processing, with no need for conversion to a different format.

Conversely, you can use it to integrate various objects from foreign systems within an Imagineer Technical container and edit them with the functions that we looked at above.

Mediator

Finally, the package can act as a bond between CAD systems and applications from the commercial areas of a company, as thanks to OLE for D&M all graphical objects are now ready for interaction with office applications of all types.

Not an alternative

Intergraph is not positioning the new system as an alternative to any of the popular 2D systems, and it does not intend to load it down with functionality to rival that of AutoCAD or MicroStation. Above all it is seen as a 2D component that practically anyone can use for a diverse range of purposes – even in desktop publishing, for example. Imagineer Technical is of course also the 2D module that will find its way into all of Intergraph's OLE-based applications.

7 Large Scale Integration

7 Large-Scale Integration

So now you know what the next generation of CAD applications has in store for you - or perhaps it would be better to say that you know what is being developed at Intergraph and what it is all based on.

What you now know

What is not yet clear is how the host of other vendors of technical software solutions will respond to this new situation. Some will presumably wait to see how OLE for D&M catches on and how widely and quickly support for this technology develops into a criterion in selection decisions.

What nobody knows

Some may quite soon come to market with suitable adaptations, in the form of OLE data servers, for example, particularly as some systems were adopting the same approach anyway.

Who's next?

This is not just a case of competition stimulating business. Unless as many application vendors as possible see this approach as the way ahead and adopt it as the basis for their own products, the true objective of OLE will never be achieved: to put an end to proprietary systems and clear the way for users to explore the wide world of open system environments.

End of an era?

It is probable, though, that the speed of adjustment will largely be decided by you, the CAD user, the engineer, the ones who really benefit from graphical software systems.

I am in no doubt that in the next few years OLE will come to be accepted as a standard technology everywhere, and that includes the field of technical applications. Consequently, Windows 95 and its successors will allow Microsoft's operating system to make the breakthrough as the standard operating system even for users in industrial product development and in the fields of GIS and architecture.

Windows on the verge of a breakthrough in CAD?

If this vision proves true, the character of the CAD world and of computer utilization in general will be

New level of integration

Figure 48: see Color Section

changed more thoroughly than by all previous generation switches in computer-aided graphics systems put together. For then for the first time there could truly be communication between all parts of a company on a common basis, using the same technology as is already prevalent within the office world today.

Getting networked

The most important issue that Microsoft has not yet resolved in this context is that of making OLE available on heterogeneous networks as well, so that the possibility of traditional and OLE-based CAD systems coexisting can be exploited in practice to protect huge company investments.

Renaissance for small design offices?

Change – for the most part welcome – is also in the air for software developers throughout the world. Unlimited availability of stable, mature components and standardized programming languages and tools will make it possible to design outstanding applications which integrate seamlessly with other products within the OLE world without vast, prohibitively expensive teams of developers.

Maybe, then, software development will again become a more rewarding business than it has been in the last five years – even if the price for systems designed in this way drops to a level considerably lower than that hitherto commanded, for example, by mammoth, all-inclusive CAD packages.

Everything takes time – OLE included

Nobody should expect all the required CAD/CAM functionality to be available in OLE-capable systems within one or even two years. The mammoths will not disappear overnight, but as in real life they will die out gradually because they no longer fit into the changed environment. Those who adapt best to the new conditions will doubtless continue longest to have a defining influence on the overall picture.

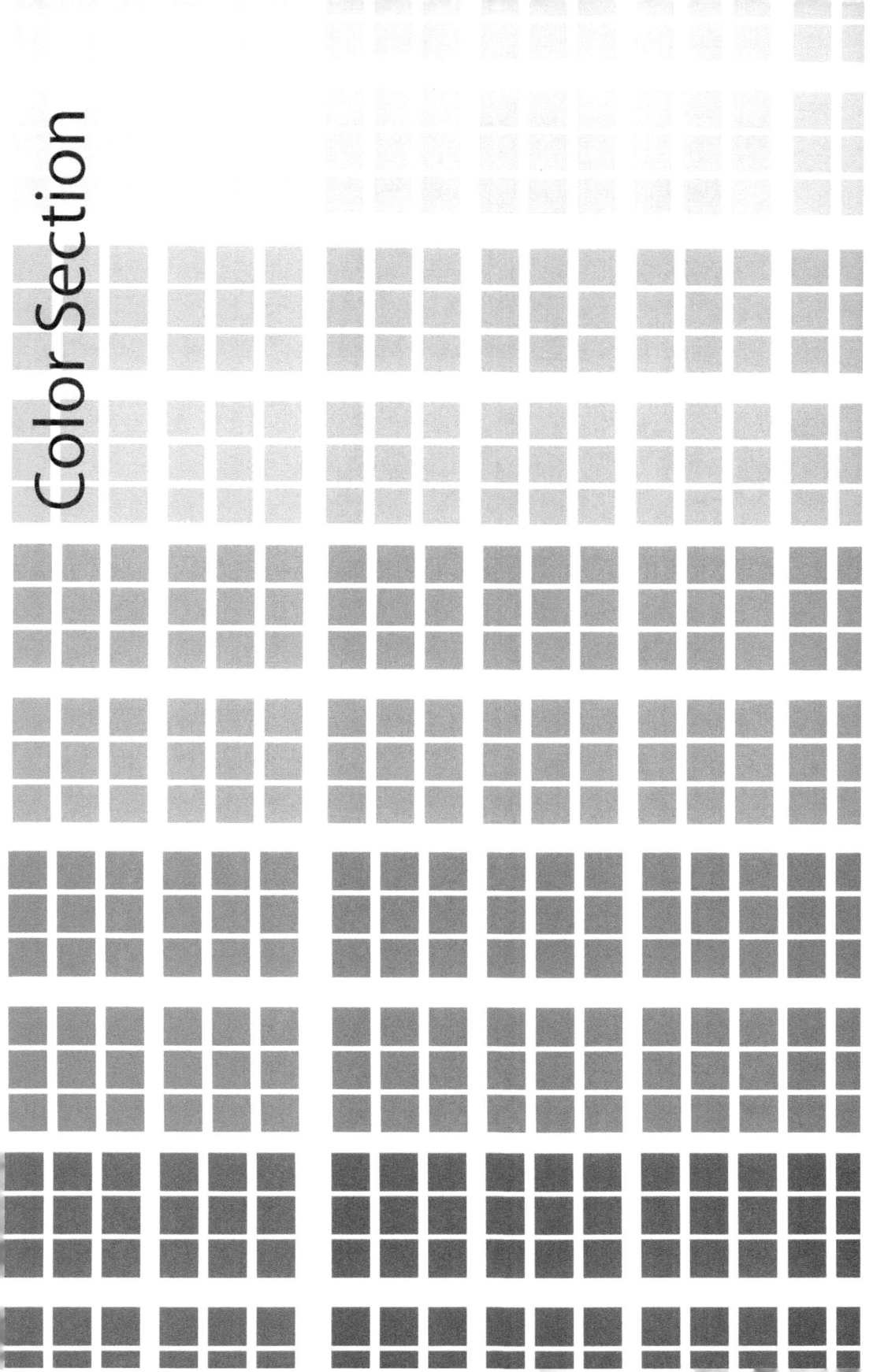

Color Section

Figure 21: "A graphic like this is largely useless as a pixel image. The information it contains is completely lost. Even simply resizing the graphic makes it unusable."

Figure 23

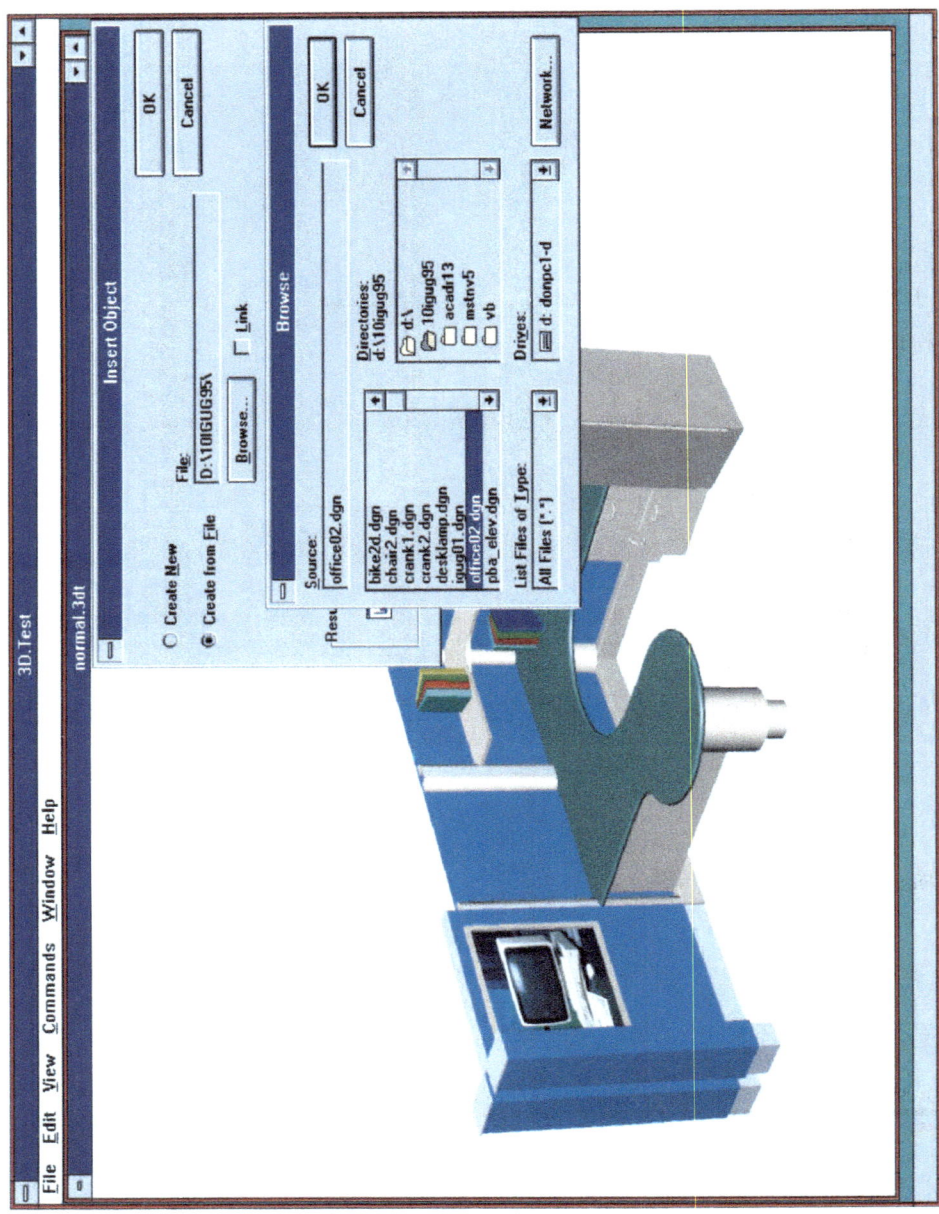

Figure 28: "Just as a 3D object can be viewed in two dimensions, the opposite is also possible, i.e. a 2D graphic may need to be placed within a 3D container. It then makes sense for it to relate to surfaces of existing objects. Here, the scanned image of a desktop computer has been positioned on one of the walls of the office."

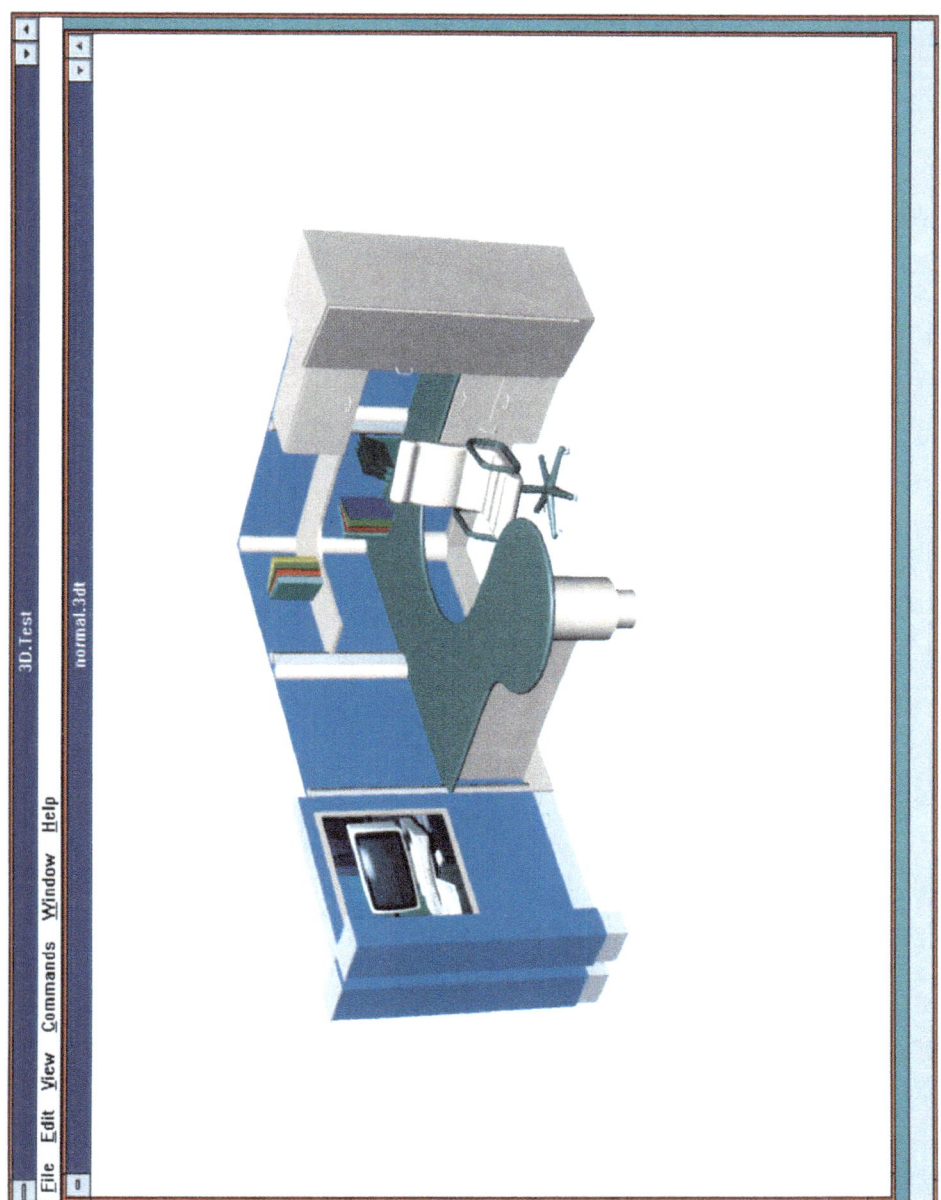

Figure 32: "Now in its foreign data structure the chair is loaded into a 3D container holding an office. The chair is positioned both in relation to the floor surface of the office and in relation to the existing elements such as the desk and the office wall. You can clearly see how 3D objects are superimposed on each other and share the space in the container: the chair is partly obscured by the shaded desktop, and it in turn obscures part of the rest of the furnishings. That would not have been possible with OLE 2."

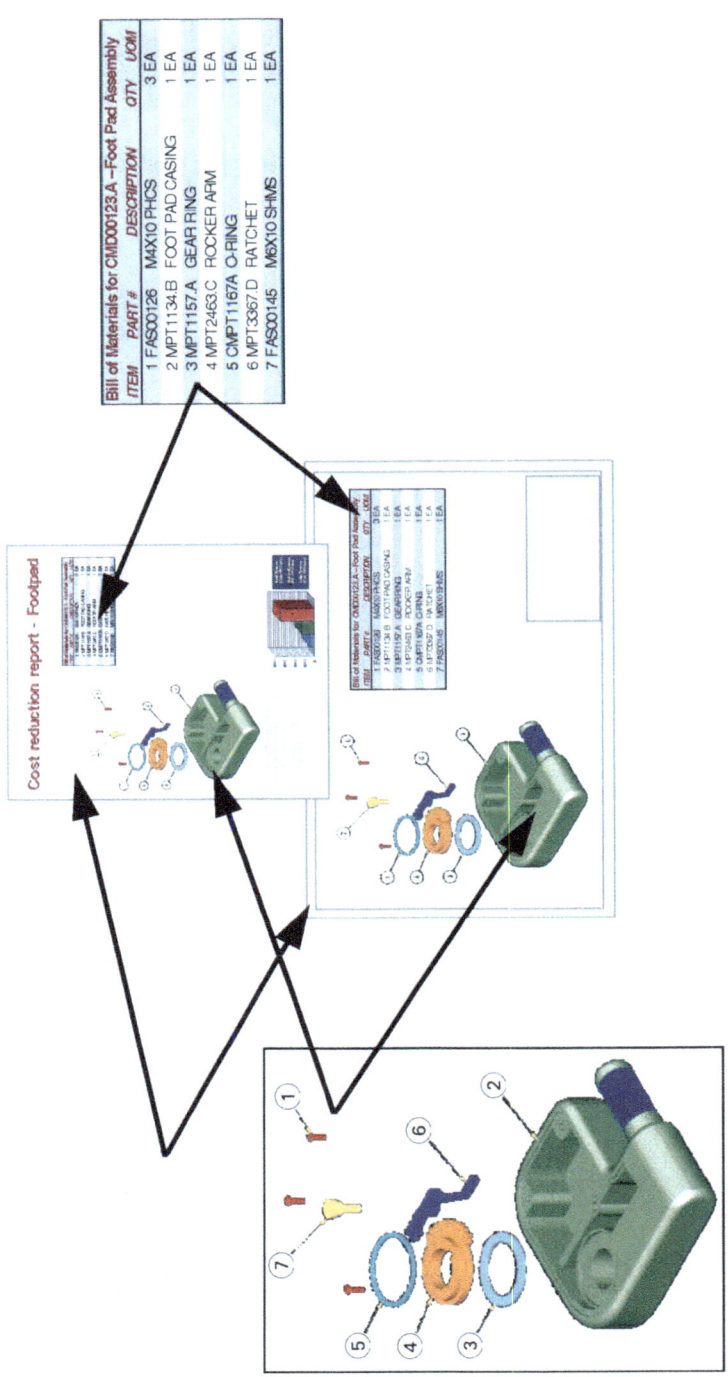

Figure 48: "This is the way things could really work before long: 3D CAD models displayed in word processors; word processors used to label drawings; spreadsheets supplying precise headers for drawings; in short, all the relevant applications can handle the same data without having to convert it first."

Appendix

"OLE for Design & Modeling Applications" Design Specification

December 8, 1995

1. Introduction

This document contains the detailed specification for the technical content of *"OLE for Design & Modeling Applications"*, an industry defined extension to OLE that enables three-dimensional compound document functionality.

Modeling applications use three dimensional entities and define relationships between these entities. Manipulations of one entity may require information about another entity to produce or maintain the correct relationship. Geometric relationships are the most obvious example but modeling applications are not limited to this. To provide interoperability between modeling applications, OLE interfaces are defined to communicate three dimensional information between objects and to allow an object to be in-place edited in the context of its overall model.

The illustration below shows graphically where the *"OLE for Design & Modeling Applications"* (*OLE D&M* for short) interfaces fit within the current set of OLE interfaces as defined by Microsoft.

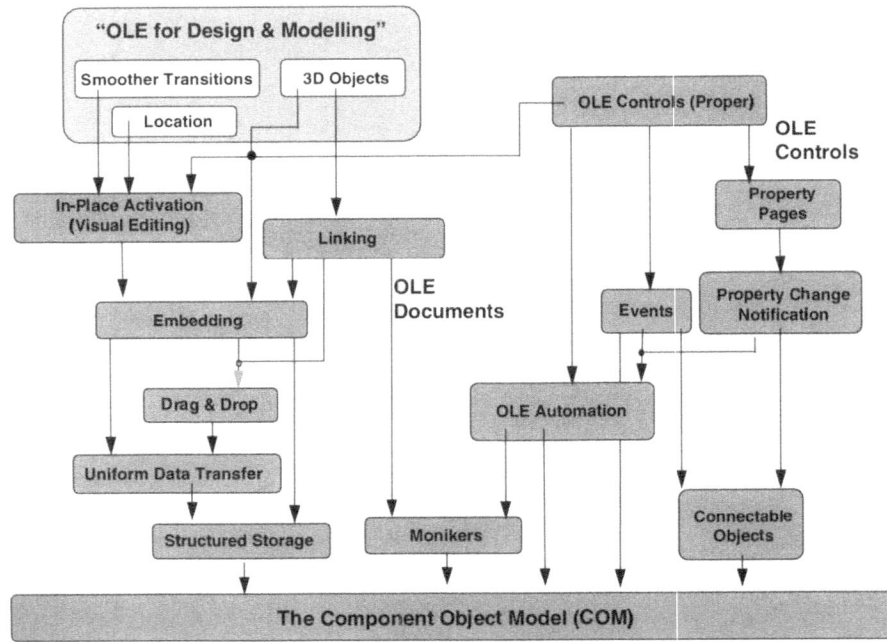

1.1. The "OLE for Design & Modeling Applications" Council

This specification has been placed in the public domain by it's original designer, Intergraph Corporation. Several vendors including Intergraph, Microsoft, and Autodesk are working to create a 'council' that can take ownership of this specification and move it forward. *"OLE for Design & Modeling Applications"* is what Microsoft calls an *OLE Industry Solution*; that is, it is a 3rd party initiative to extend OLE for a specific industry or industry segment. For more information on OLE Industry Solutions see the January 1995 issue of the Microsoft Developer Network News.

This specification resides on Microsoft's ftp server, *ftp.microsoft.com*. Log in as *anonymous* and change to the directory to: /developr/drg/OLE-Info/OLE-Industry-Solutions/Design-And-Modeling. The official definition of OLE for Design and Modeling is the include file **OLE4DM.H** which can be found in the same directory.

You'll find OLE for Design and Modeling "sample code" evolving on Intergraph's ftp server *Ftp.Intergraph.com* (129.135.1.1). Log in as *anonymous* and change to the directory *pub/win32/ole4dm*. The sample code is a zipped executable, *ole4dm??.exe, where ?? is a version number.*

You can also get to the code samples and design specs via the world-wide web: *www.intergraph.com* – look under 'Product Information' and then under Software Development Technology.

1.2. Organization of this Document

The remainder of this document contains the detailed specification for the technical content of *"OLE for Design & Modeling Applications"*. Interfaces defined fall into three major classes, each with it's own chapter (*Three Dimensional Objects, In-Place Activation*, and *Locating Pseudo-Objects*). These chapters are followed by a chapter on *User Interface*.

♦*Annotations are indicated by diamond shaped bullet points (like this one).   They are used to indicate places in the specification where additional work is needed.*

Each feature section within a chapter has the following format:

X.X. Feature Name
Priority: *Low, Medium, or High*
Stability: *Low, Medium, or High*
Overview: *Brief technical or conceptual overview of this feature, it's expected uses, known problems it solves or scenarios it enables.*

♦*Each feature should have a small code fragment that clearly illustrates it's implementation use.*

1.3. Revision History

Date	Comments
October 5, 1994	Preliminary Draft
November 30, 1994	OLE architect feedback incorporated
December 6, 1994	Additional refinements
January 19, 1995	Final Draft for Design Preview
April 9, 1995	Made following changes to specification to match OLE4DM.H file:
	Re-ordered IOleInPlaceViews' methods
	Changed Get3DExtent to GetExtent
	Added GUIDS
	Changed Draw(DVREP....) to Draw(DWORD....) & explained use of DVREP
	Changed DVREP from 1,2,4,8 to 0,1,2; can't be bitwise union
	Updated SHAPETYPE
	Added IEnumHWND interface definition
	Added DWORD repres to IOleLocate
	Added S_FALSE to IOleLocate methods returns if nothing located
	Made following changes to clarify design
	Moved IOleInPlace3DObject to section 3
	Added note on where sample code is.
	Added note on server presenting itself in meters
	Added notes on container controlling display
	Added notes on concatenated model matrices and server initializing to Identity
	Added note on Server Deactivation
	Added note on how 2D applications may be able to use model context ideas.
	Added note on using IGL interface for dynamics
	Added note on locating in chain of nested objects.
	Added note on server converting boreline to meters
May 31, 1995	Added clarifications to pVToW and pWToV matrices in IOle3DObject ::GetDefaultView, IOle3DObject ::SetView , IViewGLObject ::Draw, and IOleInPlaceViews:: GetViewContext.

Date	Comments
December 8, 1995	Addition of section regarding 2D/3D server/container combinations. Changes for support of in-place activation: Remove *IOleInPlaceActive3DObject::OnViewDelete* method. Remove *IOleInPlace3DObject interface.* Move ::OnModelMatrixChange to *IOleInPlaceActive3DObject* Replace *IOle3DObject::GetDefaultView,* and *IOle3DObject::SetView* with *IMsoDocument* interface methods. New interface method *IOleInPlaceActive3DObject::BringViewsToFront,* *IOleInPlaceActive3DObject::OnContainerRequestFocus,* and *IOleInPlaceViews::OnObjectRequestFocus.* Change parameter list of *IOleInPlaceActive3DObject::OnModelMatrixChange* Change parameter list of *IOleInPlaceViews::GetViewContext.* Change parameter list of *IOleInPlaceActive3DObject::OnInPlaceViewChange.* Enhanced section on User Interface.

2. Three Dimensional Objects

Priority: High
Stability: High

Overview: With more applications today modeling 3 dimensional phy-sical entities it becomes important to provide interfaces so that objects can communicate certain 3 dimensional information. New interfaces allow 3 dimensional containers and objects to take full advantage of the third dimension. This does not relieve them of the responsibility of working with 2 dimensional applications. The 3D container must still be able to insert 2 dimensional objects and the 3D object must still be insertable in a 2D container.

Approach: IOle3DObject is an extension of IOleObject that allows a container that understands 3 dimensions to retrieve 3 dimensional information about an object so that it may know its spatial relation to the rest of its 3 dimensional entities. IOle3DObject::GetExtent is analagous to IOleObject::GetExtent and returns the extents of the object in 3 dimensions. A 3 dimensional object must still support IOleObject::GetExtent when it is inserted into 2 dimensional containers.

The problem of deciding which view of an object to display is not unique to modeling applications, but it is a *very* special problem for them. These applications frequently wish to specify/influence the orien-tation and other characteristics of the data they display. Containers make use of Microsoft's Office Binder interfaces (IMSoDocument and IMSoView) to attach a document with a specific view.

IViewGLObject allows a 3 dimensional container to provide OpenGL dis-play capabilities to a 3 dimensional object. When an object is loaded and the container retrieves the IViewObject interface it may also query for the IViewGLObject interface. If the object supports IViewGLObject, then the container can ask the object to render itself via OpenGL. If the object does not support IViewGLObject, then the container must use IViewObject and enable a 2 dimensional display in the 3 dimensional container (the site creates a GDI to GL adapter). This specification *does not restrict 3D rendering to OpenGL and applications may define additional render-ing interfaces (IView<3DRenderer>Object).* The default, however, is

OpenGL and applications must be able to expect QueryInterface for IViewGLObject to be successful. Although IViewGLObject::Draw is analagous to IViewObject::Draw, it is completely independent of IViewObject which the object must still support in order to be displayed in a 2 dimensional container.[1]

When a 3 dimensional object is inserted into a 3 dimensional container, the 3 dimensional orientation of the object should be stored in the container site. This is called the attachment matrix. Creation and storing of this attachment matrix is up to the container and requires no OLE interface in of itself.

Another issue regarding 3 dimensional objects is how to convey their representation in a way analagous to DVASPECT. DVASPECT is an enumerator allowing you to specify standard representations for Office Automation data. These representations are CONTENT, THUMBNAIL, ICON, DOCPRINT. For 3 dimensional objects we provide an enumerator called DVREP with values of CONTENT, SIMPLIFIED, SYMBOL.

```
interface IOle3DObject : IUnknown {
    // *** IUnknown methods ***
    HRESULTQueryInterface (REFIID riid, LPVOID FAR* ppvObj);
    ULONGAddRef ();
    ULONGRelease ();
    // *** IOle3DObject methods ***
    HRESULTGetExtent (DWORD dwRep, LPEXTENT3D pExtent);
};
```

♦*Earlier versions of this specification included the methods ::GetDefaultView and ::SetView. They are made redundant/obsolete with the introduction of the Office 95 interface IMsoDocument and IMsoView interfaces.*

---

[1] Containers and objects that support 3D embedding may support "view" interfaces above and beyond IViewObject and IViewGLObject (e.g. for rendering systems other than OpenGL). In this case the container should QueryInterface on IViewObject for the new interface first, and if that fails, QueryInterface for IViewGLObject.

DEFINE_GUID(IID_IOle3DObject, 0x0002D200, 0x0000, 0x0000, 0xC0, 0x00, 0x00, 0x00, 0x00, 0x00, 0x00, 0x46);

```
interface IViewGLObject : IUnknown {
    // *** IUnknown methods ***
    HRESULTQueryInterface (REFIID riid, LPVOID FAR* ppvObj);
    ULONGAddRef ();
    ULONGRelease ();
    // *** IViewGLObject methods ***
    HRESULTDraw (DWORD dwRep, LPGL pIGL);
    };
```
♦*Earlier versions of this specification of the ::Draw method included transformations from world to view, view to world, and clipping information. This information is now included with the IGL interface and has been removed from the ::Draw method.*

DEFINE_GUID(IID_IViewGLObject,0x0002D201, 0x0000, 0x0000, 0xC0, 0x00, 0x00, 0x00, 0x00, 0x00, 0x00, 0x46);

```
typedef enum tagDVREP {          // Standard representations
    DVREP_CONTENT   = 0,         // display all the details of the object
    DVREP_SIMPLIFIED = 1,        // display a simplified version
    DVREP_SYMBOL    = 2          // display as a symbol

} DVREP;

// Extent definition
typedef double*  EXTENT3D;       // Low point, and High points (6 doubles)
typedef EXTENT3D LPEXTENT3D;
```

2.1. IOle3DObject interface

The IOle3DObject interface is implemented by 3D graphic objects and is used by 3D containers.

2.1.1. IOle3DObject::GetExtent

HRESULT IOle3DObject:: GetExtent (DWORD dwRep, LPEXTENT3D pExtent)
Returns the 3D extent of a 3D object, depending on its representation.

Argument	Type	Description
dwRep	DWORD	Type of representation requested. It is an extension of the 2D aspect of IOleObject::GetExtent. This argument may be a DVREP value but that is not required.
pExtent	LPEXTENT3D	Array of 6 doubles representing the low and high points of the object expressed in meters in the server coordinate system.
return value	S_OK	The extent is returned successfully.
E_INVALIDARG		One of the arguments is invalid.
E_OUTOFMEMORY		Out of memory.
E_UNEXPECTED		An unexpected error happened.

The immediate container sends GetExtent to the server in order to display the tracker and get the range of the object for locate/display purposes. Servers may use whatever units they desire internally but must communicate to the container in meters. Thus all containers may depend on servers in meters. The range is then transformed into the container coordinate system using the site's attachment matrix. The attachment may also account for transforming server coordinates from meters to the units of the container.

2.1.1.1. See Also   IOleObject::GetExtent

2.2. IViewGLObject interface

The IViewGLObject interface is the default 3D counterpart to the IViewObject interface. It allows 3D servers to display themselves in the container display context. This interface refers explicitly to an argument of type IGL interface which is understood to be an OpenGL COM interface that provides a "cooperative" container/server display mechanism. *OLE for Design & Modeling* container applications will generally expect an object that supports IOle3DObject to support IViewGLObject. However, the container must be prepared for the case where this interface is not supported (in which case IViewObject should be used instead).[2]

2.2.1. IViewGLObject::Draw

HRESULT IViewGLObject ::Draw (DWORD dwRep, LPGL pIGL)
Displays a server within a display context.

Argument	Type	Description
dwRep	DWORD	Type of representation requested. It is an extension of the 2D aspect of IOleObject::GetExtent.
pIGL	LPGL	Pointer to the IGL interface. To display, the server simply calls IGL functions on the IGL interface pointer. The server can call GL get functions to query information about the context.
return value	S_OK	Operation is successful.
	E_INVALIDARG	One of the arguments is invalid.
	E_UNEXPECTED	An unexpected error happened

During the display, the 3D Site pushes its attachment matrix, the eventual override symbology, transforms the clipping planes, and then asks the 3D server to display. The server determines which objects to have to be drawn using the clipping plane information available from the IGL interface and then calls functions from IGL to display itself. Note that since it presents itself to the container in meters, then it must convert its coordinates to meters prior to making the IGL calls (it can do this by pushing a scaling matrix onto the rendering context prior to displaying). Then the client pops the context back (matrix, symbology, clipping planes, and so on). The server may access the View to World matrix from IGL for view independent displays (for example, view independent text which should not display sheared, rotated or skewed). In these cases, the server may use this to reverse the container's view matrix.

[2] As noted earlier objects may also implement "view" interfaces other than IViewGLObject. For example if there exists a rendering API called XYZ, a container optimized for that API would QueryInterface on the object's IViewObject for IViewXYZObject. If that QI call failed, the container should then QI for IViewGLObject. If QI for IViewGLObject fails, the container should use IViewObject.

3. In-Place Activation

Priority: High
Stability: High
Overview: In-place activation results in user interface transitions from one active object to the next. These transitions must become smoother as more applications combine large numbers of different objects with complicated relationships in the same container/document. More objects require non-rectangular boundaries and more applications require objects to overlap but not always obscure each other (irregular polygons and transparency).

When an object becomes in-place active, 3D modeling applications prefer to work in a complete view of the model rather than a window specially created for the active object. Otherwise, it is difficult to edit the object and witness the effects on the rest of the model (and make use of the rest of the model). 3D modeling application users want to edit in the context of the container data and the other objects with which it has spatial relationships. When an object becomes in-place active, it should not change its visual relationship to the rest of the model, lest it disorient the user. The active object's menus are available for editing, but the container controls how the model is presented to the user.

For containers that provide multiple views of data (e.g. top, side, oblique), new interfaces allow objects to become in-place active in multiple views simultaneously, allowing continuous, uninterrupted editing of the object while taking advantage of and working in these disparate views.

Approach: When activated, the object asks the container for the views in which it supports in-place activation. It then creates a child view corresponding to each of those views. Each newly created child view has the same extents as the corresponding container view. These new views allow the object to receive events and perform rubberbanding, but they are otherwise unobtrusive; they are in fact, invisible. Since the active server receives all events, the default way to deactivate is via <esc> or a double-click on another object.

There is one important rule of behavior that UI-Active 3D modeling objects must follow, given that they are rendering to the container's rendering context and the container is in control of display. Even

though they are UI-Active, they do not display of their own initiative
(except dynamics/rubber-banding). The 3D modeling UI-Active object
displays in the container's original view when the container sends a
IViewGLObject::Draw (or IView<*3DRenderer*>Object). Thus, the container con-
tinually provides a complete view of the model.

The main interface facilitating this is IOleInPlaceViews to which the server
obtains a pointer via IOleInPlace3DSite::GetWindowContext.
As part of in-place activation, the server calls
IOleInPlaceViews::EnumInPlaceViews to receive a list of the container's views
supporting in-place activation. For each of these views, the server calls
IOleInPlaceViews::GetViewContext to get an IUnknown render interface pointer
and ModelView, Projection, and ViewPort matrices. The server also
creates a corresponding invisible child view that is on top. Thus, it
can properly process events and perform dynamic (rubberbanding)
displays for that view. These child views become the active views of
the server. Lastly it calls IOleInPlaceViews::SetActive3DObject to give the
document a pointer to its IOleInPlaceActive3DObject interface.
A server may utilize IOleInPlaceViews almost in place of IOleInPlaceUIWindow
(except for SetActiveObject) if it intends to control views during in-place
activation. The container must still support IOleInPlaceUIWindow for
SetActiveObject and for servers negotiating border space.
The IOleInPlaceActive3DObject interface allows the container to inform the in-
place active object of any view changes, deletions or creations.
IOleInPlace3DSite::GetModelMatrix allows the in-place active object to retrieve
the model matrix which is a concatenation of all the attachment matrices
from the outermost 3D container to the in-place server. This is because
each intermediate container in turn calls this function on its container;
the function recursing until it reaches the outermost 3D container. This
is important for the object to be able to transform events from the
outermost container's coordinate system to its coordinate system. This
is somewhat analogous to IOleInPlaceSite::GetWindowContext which returns
lprcPosRect.

IOleInPlaceActive3DObject::OnModelMatrixChange allows the container to inform
the in-place active object of changes in its 3 dimensional position and
orientation. The outermost 3 dimensional container might allow a
change to the attachment matrix (although it should not) in which case,

the container would have to call IOleInPlaceActive3dObject::OnModelMatrixChange to inform the in-place active object of the new model matrix. Upon receipt of this message, the active server should call IOleIn-Place3DSite::GetModelMatrix to get the new model matrix.
The more complete in-place activation flow is as follows: receiving IOleObject::DoVerb, the server calls:

- IOleClientSite::QueryInterface for the IOleInPlaceSite interface, and stores it.
- IOleInPlaceSite::QueryInterface for the IOleInPlace3DSite interface, and stores it.
- IOleInPlaceSite::CanInPlaceActivate, asking if the container supports In-place activation.
  IOleInPlace3DSite::GetModelMatrix to get the ModelMatrix (outermost container to server). Note that this call recurses until it reaches the outermost 3D container.
- IOleInPlaceSite::OnInPlaceActivate to notify the container that the object is about to be activated.
- IOleInPlaceSite::OnUIActivatate to notify the container that the menus are going to be merged.
- IOleInPlaceSite::GetWindowContext to return IOleInPlaceFrame and IOleInPlaceUIWindow interfaces.
- IOleInPlace3DSite::GetWindowContext to return the IOleInPlaceViews interface.
- CreateMenu to create an empty menu.
- IOleInPlaceFrame::InsertMenus   to ask the container to insert its menus.
- InsertMenus to insert its own menus.
- IOleInPlaceUIWindow::SetActiveObject to give the container a pointer to its IOleInPlaceActiveObject.
- IOleInPlaceViews::SetActive3DObject to give the container a pointer to its IOleInPlaceActive3DObject.
- IOleInPlaceViews::EnumInPlaceViews to get the list of container views.
- IOleInPlaceViews::GetViewsContext to get view context for each view.
- IOleInPlaceFrame::SetMenu to set the composite frame menu on the container's frame.

No matter how the User Interface dictates it, (as with any other OLE object) the in-place active 3D object de-activates when it receives an IOleInPlaceObject::InPlaceDeactivate or UIDeactivate message.

♦*Note that the concepts and interfaces described here are not restricted to 3D applications. Many 2D modeling applications may benefit from the same concepts . The interfaces do assume 3D coordinates and matrices, however. Refer to section 5.*

```
interface IOleInPlace3DSite  : IUnknown {
        // *** IUnknown methods ***
        HRESULTQueryInterface (REFIID riid, LPVOID FAR* ppvObj);
        ULONGAddRef ();
        ULONGRelease ();
        // *** IOleInPlace3DSite methods ***
        HRESULTGetModelMatrix (LPXFORM3D pMatrix);
        HRESULTGetWindowContext (LPOLEINPLACEVIEWS* ppInPlaceViews);
        };
DEFINE_GUID(IID_IOleInPlace3DSite,       0x0002D206, 0x0000, 0x0000, 0xC0, 0x00, 0x00,
0x00, 0x00, 0x00, 0x00, 0x46);


interface IOleInPlaceViews : IUnknown {
        // *** IUnknown methods ***
        HRESULTQueryInterface (REFIID riid, LPVOID FAR* ppvObj);
        ULONGAddRef ();
        ULONGRelease ();
        // *** IOleInPlaceViews  methods ***
        HRESULTEnumInPlaceViews (LPENUMHWND* ppenumHwnd);
        HRESULTGetViewContext  (HWND hwnd, LPUNKNOWN *pRender, LPXFORM3D
               pModelView, LPXFORM3D  pProjection, LPXFORM3D pInVProjection,
               LPVIEWPORT pViewPort);
        HRESULTSetActive3DObject( LPOLEINPLACEACTIVE3DOBJECT p3DActiveObj);
        HRESULTOnObjectRequestFocus();
        };
```

♦*Earlier versions of this specification did not include the viewport matrix as an argument to ::GetViewContext. However, it is necessary to compute the correct rendering context for rubberbanding.*

```
DEFINE_GUID(IID_IOleInPlaceViews,       0x0002D203, 0x0000, 0x0000, 0xC0, 0x00, 0x00,
0x00, 0x00, 0x00, 0x00, 0x46);


interface IOleInPlaceActive3DObject :IUnknown {
        // *** IUnknown methods ***
        HRESULTQueryInterface (REFIID riid, LPVOID FAR* ppvObj);
        ULONGAddRef ();
        ULONGRelease ();
        // *** IOleInPlaceActiveObject methods ***
        // *** IOleInPlaceActive3DObject methods ***
        HRESULTOnInPlaceViewCreate(HWND hwnd);
        HRESULTOnInPlaceViewChange(HWND hwnd);
        HRESULTOnModelMatrixChange ();
        HRESULTOnContainerRequestFocus();
        HRESULTBringViewsToFront();


}
```

♦*Earlier versions of this specification included the interface method OnInPlaceViewDelete. This method was removed because the server is a child window of the container and will receive the Window event WM_DELETE before it could ever receive this message.*

♦Earlier versions of this specification for ::OnInPlaceViewChange included pointers to the world to view and view to world transformation matrices. This information is not required to be passed for this method. Instead, if the server needs the information, it should call IOleInPlaceViews::GetViewContext.

♦Earlier versions of this specification of ::OnModelMatrixChange inlcuded a pointer to the model matrix. This is not necessary, and the server should call IOleInPlace3DSite::GetModelMatrix if the matrix is needed. This method used to be on IOleInPlace3DObject; now, it is on IOleInPlaceActive3DObject.

DEFINE_GUID(IID_IOleInPlaceActive3DObject,0x0002D204, 0x0000, 0x0000, 0xC0, 0x00, 0x00, 0x00, 0x00, 0x00, 0x00, 0x46);

```
interface IEnumHWND : IUnknown {
    // *** IUnknown methods ***
    HRESULTQueryInterface (REFIID riid, LPVOID FAR* ppvObj);
    ULONGAddRef ();
    ULONGRelease ();
    // *** IEnumHWND methods ***
    HRESULTNext (ULONG celt, _PHWND rgelt, ULONG FAR *pceltFetched);
    HRESULTSkip (ULONG celt);
    HRESULTReset ();
    HRESULTClone (IEnumHWND FAR *FAR *ppEnum);
};
DEFINE_GUID(IID_IEnumHWND,          0x0002D207, 0x0000, 0x0000, 0xC0, 0x00,
        0x00, 0x00, 0x00, 0x00, 0x00, 0x46);
// XForm matrix
typedef double* XFORM3D;        // Matrix of 16 doubles complying with GL format
typedef XFORM3D LPXFORM3D;

// Viewport definition
typedef double* VIEWPORT; // 4 doubles defining the viewport
typedef VIEWPORT LPVIEWPORT;

typedef HWND FAR* LPHWND;
typedef IEnumHWND FAR* LPENUMHWND;
```

3.1. IOleInPlace3DSite interface

The IOleInPlace3DSite interface is an extension of IOleInPlaceSite for 3D containers. It allows 3D objects to get the 3D information from the 3D containers.

3.1.1. IOleInPlace3DSite::GetModelMatrix

HRESULT IOleInPlace3DSite::GetModelMatrix (LPXFORM3D pMatrix)
Gets the transformation matrix from the in-place server to outermost 3D container.

Argument	Type	Description
pMatrix	LPXFORM3D	Pointer to an array of 16 doubles representing the 4x4 transformation from the in-place server to the outermost 3D container. This matrix is ordered in the same way as a model transformation in OpenGL. The matrix is allocated and deallocated by the caller.
return value	S_OK	The matrix is returned successfully.
	E_INVALIDARG	The argument is invalid
	E_UNEXPECTED	An unexpected error happened.

This function is called by the in-place server and recurses until it reaches the outermost 3D container, concatenating the matrices. Each object in the chain concatenates its attachment matrix to what it receives from its server (because of this, the in-place activer server should initialize the matrix to identity). It then passes this up to its container. Let us designate the outermost container's matrix M0 and all the nested intermediate container's matrices, M1 through Mn, culminating in the in-place server's which we may call S. Then, the server passes an identity matrix (S) to its container, and each intermediate container (i) concatenates its matrix (Mi) to what it receives, culminating in the outermost container's, M0. The resultant matrix product, M, is the chain M0*M1...Mi...Mn-1*Mn*S. The matrix M maps server coordinates to outermost container coordinates.

Note that the above "container's attachment matrix" refers to the attachment matrix that the container uses to orient its currently in-place active server.

See Also   IOleInPlaceActive3DObject::OnModelMatrixChange

3.1.2. IOleInPlace3DSite::GetWindowContext

HRESULT IOleInPlace3DSite :: GetWindowContext (LPOLEINPLACEVIEWS* ppInPlaceViews)

Returns the outermost 3D container window context.

Argument	Type	Description
ppInPlaceViews	LPOLEINPLACEVIEWS*	Pointer to the OleInPlaceViews interface of the outermost 3D container.
return value	SK_OK	The context is returned successfully.
	E_INVALIDARG	The argument is invalid.
	E_UNEXPECTED	An unexpected error happened.

This function recurses until it reaches the outermost 3D container and returns its IOleInPlaceViews interface to the in-place server. This function establishes the handshaking between the outermost 3D container and the 3D in-place server.

See Also   IOleInPlaceView::SetActive3DObject

3.2. IOleInPlaceViews interface

The IOleInPlaceViews interface is implemented by 3D Graphic container applications and is used by 3D Object applications to provide information about the 3D Display context. It replaces the IOleInPlaceUIWindow interface.

3.2.1. IOleInPlaceViews::EnumInPlaceViews

HRESULT IOleInPlaceViews:: EnumInPlaceViews(LPENUMHWND*
            ppenumHwnd)

Returns the list of in-place active windows into the container.

Argument	Type	Description
ppenumHwnd	LPENUMHWND*	Enumerator of the views used for in-place activation.
return value	S_OK	The Display context information is passed successfully.
	E_OUTOFMEMORY	Out of memory.
	E_INVALIDARG	One of the arguments is invalid
	E_UNEXPECTED	An unexpected error happened.

This function, implemented by 3D graphic containers, is called by In-Place 3D servers to know the list of views supporting in-place activation. Once the object has this list, it can ask for their context by calling IOleInPlaceViews::GetViewContext.

See Also   IOleInPlaceView::GetViewContext

3.2.2. IOleInPlaceViews::GetViewContext

HRESULT IOleInPlaceViews:: GetViewContext(HWND hwnd, LPUNKNOWN*
            pRender, LPXFORM3D pModelView, LPXFORM3D
            pProjection, LPXFORM3D pInVProjection, LPVIEWPORT
            pViewPort)

Returns the Graphic context of the 3D In-Place Window.

Argument	Type	Description
hwnd	HWND	Handle to the window to get context from.
pRender	LPUNKNOWN*	Address of pointer to the object that implements a rendering interface. The server must use QueryInterface this pointer using the IID of the rendering interface (usually IID_IGL).
pModelView	LPXFORM3D	Matrix representing the mapping from the outermost container's coordinate system to the outermost container's view. This matrix is a 4x4 matrix as described in OpenGL view matrices.
pProjection	LPXFORM3D	Matrix representing the projection defining the clipped viewing volume. This matrix is a 4x4 matrix as described in OpenGL view matrices.
pInVProjection	LPXFORM3D	Inverse of the projection matrix. Difficult for server to compute and thus is should be passed in.
pViewPort	LPVIEWPORT	Viewport – High and Low pixel extent of the view.
return value	S_OK	The Display context information is passed successfully.
	E_OUTOFMEMORY	Out of memory.
	E_INVALIDARG	One of the arguments is invalid
	E_UNEXPECTED	An unexpected error happened.

This function, implemented by 3D graphic containers, is called by
In-Place 3D servers to initialize their display context. At this point the
rendering interface does not have the model matrix incorporated. The
server creates a context for each of its child views and must push the
container's model matrix (see IOleInPlace3DSite::GetModelMatrix) onto the

context before displaying in dynamics. The In-Place 3D servers uses this newly created context only for dynamics (rubberbanding). It performs regular display in the container's original view when the container sends an IViewGLObject::Draw (or IView<3DRenderer>Object).

See Also   IOleInPlaceActive3DObject::OnViewMatrixChange, IOleInPlaceViews ::EnumInPlaceViews

3.2.3. IOleInPlaceViews::SetActive3DObject

HRESULT IOleInPlaceViews::SetActive3DObject
            (LPOLEINPLACEACTIVE3DOBJECT p3DActiveObj)
Sets the IOleInPlaceActive3DObject connection.

Argument	Type	Description
p3DActiveObj	LPOLEINPLACEACTIVE3DOBJECT	Pointer to the IOleInPlaceViews interface
retun value	S_OK	The operation was successful.
	E_INVALIDARG	The argument is invalid.
	E_UNEXPECTED	An unexpected error happened.

To establish a direct link between the In-Place server and the container, the server calls IOleInPlace3DSite::GetWindowContext and stores it, then it calls IOleInPlaceViews::SetActive3DObject giving its interface to IOleInPlaceActive3DObject, so the container can store its connection too.

See Also   IOleInPlace3DSite::GetWindowContext

3.2.4. IOleInPlaceViews::OnObjectRequestFocus

HRESULT IOleInPlaceViews::OnObjectRequestFocus()
Warns the container that it is about to lose focus.

When the UI-Active server gets an event in its Frame window while the container had the focus, it sends IOleInPlaceViews::OnObjectRequestFocus to warn that the container is about to lose focus. This is important if the container has taken the focus with IOleInPlaceActive3DObject::OnContainerRequestFocus to run a container view command. The container can perform cleanup on any commands prior to surrendering focus. It then sends IOleInPlaceActive3DObject::BringViewsToFront to give the focus to the server.

See Also   IOleInPlaceActive3DObject::OnContainerRequestFocus,
                    IOleInPlaceActive3DObject::BringViewsToFront

3.3. IOleInPlaceActive3DObject interface

The IOleInPlaceActive3DObject interface is an extension of IOleInPlaceActiveObject and is implemented by servers wishing to track the container's views during in-place activation. It is called by containers supporting In-Place Activation. The IOleInPlaceActive3DObject interface adds methods to notify the In-Place Active Object of changes in views.

3.3.1. IOleInPlaceActive3DObject::OnInPlaceViewCreate

HRESULT IOleInPlaceActive3DObject::OnInPlaceViewCreate(HWND hwnd)
Notifies the In-Place Object that the outermost 3D container just created a new in-place active window.

Argument	Type	Description
hwnd	HWND	Handle of view created.
return value	S_OK	The notification is received successfully.
	E_INVALIDARG	The argument is invalid.
	E_UNEXPECTED	An unexpected error happened.

The in-place server then calls IOleInPlaceViews::GetViewContext to get the new display context and stores it.

See Also   IOleInPlaceViews::GetViewContext

3.3.2. IOleInPlaceActive3DObject::OnInPlaceView Change

HRESULT IOleInPlaceActive3DObject::OnInPlaceViewChange(HWND hwnd)
Notifies the In-Place Object that the outermost 3D container modified one of its In-place views.

Argument	Type	Description
hwnd	HWND	Handle of view which was modified
return value	SK_OK	The operation was successful.
	E_INVALIDARG	The argument is invalid.
	E_UNEXPECTED	An unexpected error happened.

The in-place server has to update the view information by calling
IOleInPlaceViews::GetViewContext.

See Also   IOleInPlaceViews::GetViewContext; IOleInPlace3DSite::GetModelMatrix

3.3.3. IOleInPlaceActive3DObject:OnContainerRequestFocus

HRESULT IOleInPlaceActive3DObject ::OnContainerRequestFocus ()
Sent by the container to the active server to warn it that it is about to
lose focus.

Before the container starts a view command, it sends
IOleInPlaceActive3DObject::OnContainerRequestFocus to the active
server to warn it that it is about to lose focus. The server can perform
cleanup of any active commands before surrendering focus and stores
its new state.

See Also   IOleInPlaceViews::OnObjectRequestFocus,
                    IOleInPlaceActive3DObject::BringViewsToFront

3.3.4. IOleInPlaceActive3DObject::BringViewsToFront

HRESULT IOleInPlaceActive3DObject ::BringViewsToFront ()
Brings the active servers invisible child views back to the front so the
server can process events.

After the container completes a view command, it should return focus
to the active server by sending
IOleInPlaceActive3DObject::BringViewsToFront. While running a
command, if the container receives
IOleInPlaceViews::OnObjectRequestFocus, it performs cleanup and
then gives the server focus by sending
IOleInPlaceActive3DObject::BringViewsToFront.

See Also   IOleInPlaceViews::OnObjectRequestFocus,
                   IOleInPlaceActive3DObject::OnContainerRequestFocus

3.3.5. IOleInPlaceActive3DObject::OnModelMatrixChange

HRESULT IOleInPlaceActive3DObject ::OnModelMatrixChange ()
Notifies the in-place object that the outermost 3D container changed its model transformation matrix.

Argument	Type	Description
return value	S_OK	The notification is done sucessfully.
	E_OUTOFMEMORY	Out of memory.
	E_UNEXPECTED	An unexpected error happened.

The server then gets the new model matrix by calling IOleInPlace3DSite::GetModelMatrix.

See Also   IOleInPlace3DSite::GetModelMatrix

3.4. IEnumHWND interface

The IEnumHWND interface is a standard Enumerator interface for HWNDS and is implemented by containers and used by 3D graphic objects to iterate through a list of container HWNDs. It follows the standard Enumerator protocol outlined in the OLE 2.0 Design Specification.

4. Locating Pseudo-Objects

Priority: High
Stability: High
Overview: As applications combine objects with complicated relation-ships in a container/document, it seems reasonable that one object may make use of information in another object.
This is not just "dragging" one object into another object container. That interoperability extends to sharing the container space and the user's time/attention. This allows one object to "find" another object. What is done with that information is up to the user or server applica-tion. But it allows overlapping objects to utilize each other's position and geometry during complicated, precise-relationship manipulations.
Approach: The IOleLocate interface allows one to locate pseudo-objects from other objects.
The common example involves a user wanting to manipulate some geometric element relative to the geometry of some other object (or element in the container).
The container can achieve this by sending IOleLocate::PointLocate or ShapeLocate with a geometric locate criteria to the object. The UI-Active server can achieve this by sending IOleLocate::PointLocate or ShapeLocate with a geometric locate criteria to the container which behaves in this case like a server. The object can respond to this by determining what pieces of it (object, pseudo-objects, elements) meet the locate criteria. Items that meet the criteria are returned as a list of monikers.
The server or container may then call the BindMoniker helper function or IMoniker::BindToObject to bind to each moniker. If the moniker represents an OLE object, then the initiating server/container may send IOleLocate to it, and (continuing the process) achieve a nested locate into a chain of inserted OLE objects. Having bound a moniker, the server or container may retrieve a DataObject for it and make use of its geometry. It could present this in a manner allowing the user to choose how the manipulated element should relate geometrically to the located pseudo-object. The server supporting the location of pseudo-objects with IOleLocate must insure that IOleItemContainer::QueryInterface can return IOleLocate. IOleLocate must also have a pointer to IOleItemContainer to take advantage of EnumObjects and ParseDisplayName. If the server only supports location of the object itself, then IOleLocate need not be concerned with IOleItemContainer.

Note that the container must transform the boreline locate criteria to the server's coordinate system via the inverse of the attachment matrix. The server, upon receiving the boreline, must convert it from meters to its own units. When generating a data object in response to a BindMoniker, the server must present its data in meters.

```
interface IOleLocate : IUnknown {
    // *** IUnknown methods ***
    HRESULTQueryInterface (REFIID riid, LPVOID FAR* ppvObj);
    ULONGAddRef ();
    ULONGRelease ();
    // *** IOleLocate methods ***
    HRESULTPointLocate (DWORD repres, LPBORELINE pBoreLine,
        LPENUMMONIKER* ppEnumMoniker);
    HRESULTShapeLocate (DWORD repres , LPSHAPE pShape, LPENUMMONIKER*
        ppEnumMoniker);
    };
DEFINE_GUID(IID_IOleLocate   ,0x0002D202, 0x0000, 0x0000, 0xC0, 0x00, 0x00, 0x00, 0x00,
0x00, 0x00, 0x46);

typedef struct tagBoreLine {       // BoreLine definition
    double m_point[3];             // Eye Point
    double m_direction[3];         // Direction vector
    double m_front;                // Front curvilinear abscissa >= 0.0
    double m_back;                 // Back curvilinear abscissa <= 0.0
    double m_radius;               // Tolerance to locate > 0.0
    } BORELINE;
typedef  BORELINE FAR* LPBORELINE;
```

```
typedef enum tagSHAPETYPE {          // Possible types of shapes
    SHAPETYPE_INSIDE  = 1,           // Select the elements inside the polygon
    SHAPETYPE_OVERLAP = 2            // select elements overlapping either INSIDE or
        OUTSIDE
} SHAPETYPE;

typedef struct tagShape   {          // Shape definition
    double*  m_lpoint;               // List of points defining the polygon
    int      m_pointCount;           // Number of points in the list
    double   m_direction[3];         // Direction vector (of shape walls)
    double   m_front;                // Front curvilinear abscissa >= 0.0
    double   m_back;                 // Back curvilinear abscissa <= 0.0
    DWORD m_type;                    //bitwise union of SHAPETYPE
```

	//Value	Bit0	Bit1	Meaning
//	0	0	0	Select elements outside the polygon.
//	1	1	0	Select elements inside the polygon.
//	2	0	1	Select elements outside and overlapping the polygon.
//	3	1	1	Select elements inside and overlapping the polygon.

```
} SHAPE;
typedef SHAPE FAR* LPSHAPE;
```

4.1. IOleLocate interface

The IOleLocate interface is an extension of IOleItemContainer. It adds the capability of retreiving an object by a locate operation.

4.1.1. IOleLocate::PointLocate

HRESULT lOleLocate:: PointLocate (DWORD repres , LPBORELINE pBoreLine,
        LPENUMMONIKER* ppEnumMoniker)

Gets a list of all elements of an object that intersect with a point or a boreline

Argument	Type	Description
repres	DWORD	Type of representation requested. It is an extension of the 2D aspect of IOleObject:GetExtent. This argument is a DVREP value.
pBoreLine	LPBORELINE	Point + depth information to define a sphere or a cylinder used for the intersection criteria. This is a pointer to a boreline structure.
ppEnumMoniker	LPENUMMONIKER*	Moniker enumerator. Each element located is a moniker. NULL if nothing located.
return value	S_OK	One or more objects were located.
	E_OUTOFMEMORY	Out of memory.
	E_INVALIDARG	One of the arguments is invalid.
	E_UNEXPECTED	An unexpected error happened.
	S_FALSE	Nothing located.

Returns an enumerator of monikers. This moniker can be converted to a DataObject.

See Also   IOleLocate::ShapeLocate

4.1.2. IOleLocate::ShapeLocate

HRESULT IOleLocate:: ShapeLocate (DWORD repres, LPSHAPE pShape,
         LPENUMMONIKER* ppEnumMoniker)

Gets a list of all elements intersecting/contained by a shape.

Argument	Type	Description
repres	DWORD	Type of representation requested. It is an extension of the 2D aspect of IOleObject:GetExtent. This argument is a DVREP value.
pShape	LPSHAPE	Shape defined by a set of points defining a polygon, a depth and an attribute specifying the position of the object relative to this shape.
ppEnumMoniker		LPENUMMONIKER* Moniker enumerator. Each element

		located is a moniker. NULL if nothing located.
return value	S_OK	One or more objects were located.
	E_OUTOFMEMORY	Out of memory.
	E_INVALIDARG	One of the arguments is invalid.
	E_UNEXPECTED	An unexpected error happened.
	S_FALSE	Nothing located.

Return an enumerator of monikers. This moniker can be converted to a DataObject.

See Also   **IOleLocate::PointLocate**

5. 2D/3D Container/Server Combinations

The bulk of this paper addresses using OLE for Design and Modeling to insert 3D objects into 3D containers. The interfaces are designed to handle this situation. Some of these concepts are useful in strictly 2D applications as well as mixtures of 2D and 3D.

5.1. 2D Server in 2D Container

Concepts in OLE for Design and Modeling most useful to strictly 2D applications are the seamless In-Place Activation and Locate. The 3 dimensional aspects of IOle3DObject and the OpenGL characteristics of IViewGLObject and IGL are of little interest. Instead, IOleObject and IViewObject are sufficient.

5.1.1. Insertion

Insertion is done in the normal OLE2 way.

5.1.2. In-Place Activation

This is exactly the same as for 3d to 3d except that the arguments are truncated for 2d. The render interface pointer sent in IOleInPlaceViews::GetViewContext can be NULL. The server can simulate the view's DC with the supplied matrices.

5.1.3. Locate

This is similar to the 3D case; again except that the arguments are truncated for 2D.

5.2. 2D server in 3D container

5.2.1. Insertion

One of the first things a 3D OLE for Design and Modeling container does when inserting an object is to ask the server if it supports IOle3DObject. If a 2D server does support IOle3DObject, then it is its responsibility to behave completely as 3D, providing zero for z.

5.2.2. In-Place Activation

This is the same as the 3D in 3D case. It is the 2D server's responsibility to appropriately process the 3D arguments.

If the activating server does not support OLE for Design and Modeling interfaces, then the object activates in the OLE2 manner.

5.2.3. Locate

The only case addressed is where the 3d boreline locate intersects the surface/plane of the 2d server in one place.

5.3. 3D Server in 2D Container

5.3.1. Insertion

The 2d container inserts the objects as an OLE2 object.

5.3.2. In-Place Activation

If the 2D container does not support OLE for Design and Modeling interfaces, then the server activates in the traditional OLE2 way. If it does support OLE for Design and Modeling interfaces, OLE for Design and Modeling in-place activation is performed.

5.3.3. Locate

The 2D container, upon sending IOleLocate is sending to a view that is attached as 2D. Upon binding the moniker, the 2D container can receive 2D data from the DataObject, since the 3D server is projecting a 2D view.

6. User Interface

This section describes the user interface specification for actions that are specific to 3D manipulation.

Deactivating in-place active OLE for Design and Modeling Objects is done with <esc> or double-clicking another object.

In-place active OLE for Design and Modeling Objects should be indicated by greying the symbology (color) of the remaining model.

The UI-activating OLE for Design and Modeling Object does not negotiate borders in order to fit the object in the window.

Large models with many objects require in-place activation of links. This is an extension supported by OLE for D&M that was not present in OLE 2.

It is up to the Application to make the distinction between locating the entire OLE for Design and Modeling Object and locating pseudo-objects within it.

7. Appendix A - Assigned GUIDs

The "OLE for Design & Modeling Applications" specification has been allocated a range of 256 globally unique identifiers (GUIDs).   The range is {0002D2xx-0000-0000-C000-000000000046}.   This range is to be used by this specification only.

// Display-Locate interfaces

DEFINE_GUID(IID_IOle3DObject, 0x0002D200, 0x0000, 0x0000, 0xC0, 0x00, 0x00, 0x00, 0x00, 0x00, 0x00, 0x46);
DEFINE_GUID(IID_IViewGLObject,0x0002D201, 0x0000, 0x0000, 0xC0, 0x00, 0x00, 0x00, 0x00, 0x00, 0x00, 0x46);
DEFINE_GUID(IID_IOleLocate   ,0x0002D202, 0x0000, 0x0000, 0xC0, 0x00, 0x00, 0x00, 0x00, 0x00, 0x00, 0x46);

// In-Place Activation

DEFINE_GUID(IID_IOleInPlaceViews,   0x0002D203, 0x0000, 0x0000, 0xC0, 0x00, 0x00, 0x00, 0x00, 0x00, 0x00, 0x46);
DEFINE_GUID(IID_IOleInPlaceActive3DObject,0x0002D204, 0x0000, 0x0000, 0xC0, 0x00, 0x00, 0x00, 0x00, 0x00, 0x00, 0x46);
DEFINE_GUID(IID_IOleInPlace3DSite,   0x0002D206, 0x0000, 0x0000, 0xC0, 0x00, 0x00, 0x00, 0x00, 0x00, 0x00, 0x46);
DEFINE_GUID(IID_IEnumHWND,   0x0002D207, 0x0000, 0x0000, 0xC0, 0x00, 0x00, 0x00, 0x00, 0x00, 0x00, 0x46);

8. Appendix B - Structures

This sections contains a complete listing of new structures and typedefs defined for OLE for Design and Modeling Applications.

```
typedef enum tagDVREP {              // Standard representations
    DVREP_CONTENT   = 0,             // display all the details of the object
    DVREP_SIMPLIFIED = 1,            // display a simplified version
    DVREP_SYMBOL    = 2,             // display as a symbol
    } DVREP;

// Extent definition
typedef double* EXTENT3D;            // Low point, and High points (6 doubles)
typedef EXTENT3D LPEXTENT3D;

// Clipping plane equations
typedef double* CLIPPLANEEQUATION; // 6 plane equations complying with GL format
        (24 doubles)
typedef  CLIPPLANEEQUATION LPCLIPPLANES;

// XForm matrix
typedef double* XFORM3D;             // Matrix of 16 doubles complying with GL format
typedef XFORM3D LPXFORM3D;

typedef HWND FAR* LPHWND;
typedef IEnumHWND FAR* LPENUMHWND;

typedef struct tagBoreLine {         // BoreLine definition
    double m_point[3];               // Eye Point
    double m_direction[3];           // Direction vector
    double m_front;                  // Front curvilinear abscissa >= 0.0
    double m_back;                   // Back curvilinear abscissa <= 0.0
    double m_radius;                 // Tolerance to locate > 0.0
    } BORELINE;
typedef  BORELINE FAR* LPBORELINE;
```

```
typedef enum tagSHAPETYPE {        // Possible types of shapes
    SHAPETYPE_INSIDE  = 1,         // Select the elements inside the polygon
    SHAPETYPE_OVERLAP = 2          // select elements overlapping either INSIDE or
        OUTSIDE
} SHAPETYPE;


typedef struct tagShape   {        // Shape definition
    double*  m_lpoint;             // List of points defining the polygon
    int      m_pointCount;         // Number of points in the list
    double   m_direction[3];       // Direction vector (of shape walls)
    double   m_front;              // Front curvilinear abscissa >= 0.0
    double   m_back;               // Back curvilinear abscissa <= 0.0
    DWORD m_type;                  //bitwise union of SHAPETYPE
```

	//Value	Bit0	Bit1	Meaning
//	0	0	0	Select elements outside the polygon.
//	1	1	0	Select elements inside the polygon.
//	2	0	1	Select elements outside andoverlapping the polygon.
//	3	1	1	Select elements inside and overlapping the polygon.

```
    } SHAPE;
typedef SHAPE FAR* LPSHAPE;
```

Glossary

algorithm:
A term borrowed from mathematics to describe a set of computations executed in a defined sequence to perform a particular task.

associativity:
Automatic maintenance and updating of relationships between objects.

benchmark:
A performance test, in industry also used as the basis for system selection decisions. Generally involves submitting common or typical parts produced by the prospective client as examples so as to observe how the tested systems perform in a practical application.

CAS.CADE/SF:
Name of the object-oriented development platform on which Matra Datavision is basing all new developments. No exclusive commitment to Windows NT.

COM:
Component Object Model. The name of the fundamental object type in Microsoft terminology.

constraint:
In the CAD context constraints are conditions or parameters which govern geometric elements and must be observed at all times.

DOS:
Original operating system for the PC. The evolution of Windows into an operating system in its own right is making DOS superfluous.

embedding:
In the OLE context embedding involves making a copy of an object as opposed to making a *link* to it.

encapsulation:
In object technology refers to the basic principle of object formation: wrapping up data and methods as a shielded unit in which they cannot be modified or destroyed from outside.

event-driven:
Key press, mouse click and *mouse motion* are events used to control software functions directly. For example: the sequence of events "click" on file icon, drag icon onto printer icon and drop" causes the file to be sent to the printer.

features:
Design elements which are capable of understanding and maintaining their own boundary conditions.

GIS:
Short for Geographical Information System. Software used primarily in surveying. Special application domain for CAD.

interface:
In object technology refers to the specifications that allow object information to be exchanged in specific environments.

interoperability:
Refers to the ability of disparate systems from different vendors and with different data structures and programming methodologies to create or edit a common document under a common user interface.

link:
Linking among other things refers to the process of merging the parts of a system to produce an executable version. In the OLE context a link is a connection between an object and the application which created it.

Microsoft Office:
The name under which Microsoft has for some years been marketing software packages combining special-purpose products which have been integrated on the basis of the OLE mechanism; the products include Word, PowerPoint and Access.

native format:
Refers to the data format in which the elements of an application are created by default, e.g. *.DOC for Word, *.DWG for AutoCAD and so on.

OS/2:
Operating system for PS/2 systems and the PowerPC. Originally devised as the successor to DOS, OS/2 has developed into the most significant competing product, not comparable with the Microsoft system in terms of mass distribution, but more advanced in terms of user-friendliness - at least until Windows 95 was released.

PELORUS:
Name of the object-oriented software technology that Computervision is using as the basis for future technical applications. With STEP-compatible data structure and no exclusive commitment to Windows NT.

persistence:
In object technology refers to the security of data in objects.

polymorphism:
In object technology refers to the mechanism whereby individual objects respond differently to the same message.

procedure, procedural software:
A *procedure* is a section of a program, typically a named sequence of statements which performs a single task. The term *procedural software* is now used to refer to a deterministic programming technique based on clearly

defined algorithms designed to force specific actions to be performed – as distinct from object-oriented programming.

proprietary:
Privately owned; in software engineering refers to the exclusive association of functionality with hardware and/ or software platforms from a single vendor.

wrapper:
In the OLE context refers to a "shield" used to enclose a software component whose original structure is not OLE-capable.

Index

A

B

C

D

E

F

G

I

J

L

M

P

Q

R

S

T

U

V

W

Z

Printing: Mercedesdruck, Berlin
Binding: Buchbinderei Lüderitz & Bauer, Berlin